TESTIMONIALS

"Sarah's advice definitely helped make a happy ME and an even happier WE"

—Gary Plummer, 49ers, retired, Super Bowl XXIX

"Sarah had an innate ability to figure out what I was struggling with, and articulated in a natural, understandable way strategies for addressing, correcting, and improving those things. All of my time with Sarah was beneficial, and allowed me to build the life I was looking for."

—Mark C. Attorney at Law

"Sarah Ruggera is an amazing therapist. Read this book to make your relationship better and your life happier! If your relationship needs help, then please don't wait. Sarah is compassionate, effective and a joy to know and work with. Sarah will help you get to the core of the issue, listen easily to both points of view and help you get to the relationship you want and deserve."

—Casey Truffo, Author "From Clinician To Confident CEO" and Licensed Marriage and Family Therapist Orange County Relationship Center

"Sarah Ruggera helped me realize that I am also an individual in my relationship. That my relationship became better as I worked on myself and realized what I was doing to contribute the good and the bad. As a result, my husband also did the same and we now have a more mature working relationship filled with good communication and more love for one another. She is an excellent couples counselor and I highly recommend her services."

—Ashley T. Investigative Journalist

"When it comes to needing a Hail Mary pass, Sarah is a miracle worker. Her book helped me understand it was Me who needed to do the work to remain in my marriage. As a result my wife and I have a marriage I could have only dreamed about. *Happy Me Happy We* hits the nail on the head."

—Brian F., Encinitas, CA

"Sarah Ruggera was able to work with me using traditional responses as well as techniques tailored to my individual situation. She was not afraid to challenge my ingrained way of looking at things to help me instead achieve normalized results. Sarah gave me the tools to finalize my decision to divorce and put my actions into perspective relative to their influence upon my life and the lives of my children. As a result, I was able to communicate positively, directly, and openly with my children, my ex-wife, and my new life partner."

—BW, Accountant and Business Owner

HAPPY ME HAPPY WE

Six steps to know yourself so you know what you want in a relationship

SARAH RUGGERA

Ruggera Publishing

Happy Me Happy We
Six steps to know yourself so you know what you want in a relationship
Published by Ruggera Publishing

Ruggera Publishing
5230 Carroll Canyon Rd, San Diego, CA 92121
E-mail: Sarah@RuggeraPublishing.com

Publishing and editorial team:
Author Bridge Media, www.AuthorBridgeMedia.com
Project Manager and Editorial Director: Helen Chang
Publishing Manager: Laurie Aranda
Cover Designer: Mark Gelotte

Library of Congress Control Number: 2020910321

ISBN: 978-1-7351110-0-1 – softcover
978-1-7351110-1-8 – ebook

Ordering Information:

Quantity sales. Special discounts are available on quantity purchases by corporations, associations, and others. For details, contact the publisher at the address above.

Printed in the United States of America

DEDICATION

This book is dedicated to those I've helped to become the differentiated individuals they needed to be—and to those of you who want the same. In becoming that differentiated person, you will come to know yourself, so you know what you want in your relationships. Life can be everything you want, but it starts with you.

I also dedicate this book to the loves of my life: Jackie and Rachel, who make life worth living, and Phil, whose unconditional love keeps me grounded.

Contents

Acknowledgments ix

Foreword xi

Introduction 1

Overview The Roles No Longer Apply 11

Chapter 1 Intuition 31

Chapter 2 Courage 47

Chapter 3 Emotions 60

Chapter 4 Insight 76

Chapter 5 Boundaries and Groundedness 88

Chapter 6 Choices 109

Chapter 7 Your Relationship Destiny 128

About the Author 138

ACKNOWLEDGMENTS

Happy Me Happy We is a project that includes a process of enlightenment for me, my journey to becoming individuated and differentiated. For over twenty years, it's been incredibly gratifying to help others through that process to their own "light bulb" moment.

I thank my husband, Phil, for coming into my life. You're the lightning rod I need when I turn into that bolt of lightning, dishing out controversy and strong negative feelings. Thank you for loving me even when I'm not loveable. Your understanding and patience help me stay focused so I can be the best version of me. I appreciate your help and insight with my book.

I thank my daughter Jackie, who was part of my differentiation process, as I was essentially growing up while raising her. I thank you for being brave and steadfast during our journey. You have reaped the benefits of becoming better attuned to knowing how to get what you want, as will every generation that comes after you.

I thank my daughter Rachel, who, though the youngest in the family, has behaved so maturely, making parenting her an absolute joy. I appreciate your calm disposition, which helps me become more grounded, as patience is not part of my DNA. You inspired me to finish my book after many years of procrastination because of your own talent for creating stories. You make me a better person.

Thank you to my parents, who were open-minded and willing to understand and accept that the next generation's legacy is the power to make their own choices and live the life they want. Thank you to my sister, Annabelle. I admire your perseverance in life, as you've made some very good choices, making for a wonderful family of your own. And to my late brother, Sal: your untimely death provided me with so much perspective. I can live the rest of my life accepting this was the path I had to undergo to get the life that works for me. You were definitely part of that whole process.

A big thank you to the Author Bridge Media team, led by Helen Chang, my editor, who kept me focused with kind encouragement and support.

And finally, special thanks to my publishing manager, Laurie Aranda, who is fondly known to me as Laurie Jane and who happened to be my flower girl in my first wedding. A one-of-a-kind individual, Laurie made the book-publishing process even more special for me.

FOREWORD

My name is Gary Plummer, and I was fortunate enough to play fifteen years of professional football. By the time I was in my fourteenth season, I experienced headaches almost daily, and it felt like someone was driving a metal stake into the back of my head.

Ignoring pain and discomfort was a learned skill, as nothing is more revered in professional football than toughness. As I learned quickly, "it's just part of the game" is a mantra that most players live by. And so I ignored the headaches as if they were any other football injury to be endured.

When I read about Dave Duerson (hard-hitting Super Bowl champion with the Chicago Bears) and the symptoms he experienced prior to his suicide—depression, irritability, and anxiety—I related to his suffering. I had those symptoms too. But as most football players do, I quickly pushed them as far from my mind as I could. Over the next few years, other NFL players would commit suicide. Meanwhile, my symptoms of depression, irritability, and anxiety were intensifying, and I believe they ultimately contributed to my marriage ending in divorce. Things around me were changing, and I found myself incapable of processing and handling everything the way I once did.

It wasn't until May 2, 2012, when Junior Seau's suicide was announced, that I realized my story would likely come to a similar end if I didn't get help.

Junior, one of the best linebackers to ever play the game, was like a little brother to me. He was family. The last time I saw Junior was at a charity golf tournament about ten days before his death, and he was his typical outgoing and jovial self. Having mentored him during his first four years as a San Diego Charger, I took my role as his pseudo big brother seriously. I too came across as outgoing and jovial and therefore recognized in him that same discontent, deep within, he was trying so hard to ignore. When the news broke about his death, I was absolutely devastated. Could I have done more? Could I have said something different? Would it have made a difference?

Why was I willing to help my brother, but not myself?

My wife, Corey, came home from work about three hours after the news broke, and I was still sitting in the same position—on the exercise bike in our home gym, in front of the TV, tears streaming down my face. The rest of the day was a blur of interviews discussing the enormous loss that had rocked the football community and its fans.

The following morning, Corey called Sarah, who skipped her usual greeting and said, "I've been waiting for you to call. I've cleared my schedule. When can you bring him in?"

Corey informed me I was scheduled to see Sarah that morning, and when my response was a dismissive facial expression, Corey said, her voice shaking, "I can't have you be next." With those words, I knew that I could no longer allow toughness to be my compass through life.

Corey joined the session long enough to divulge that she too was worried about the ongoing symptoms I was exhibiting. After sharing her observations, she provided Sarah and me with the privacy we needed to address my sadness and devastation over the loss of someone I loved dearly and the mixed bag of emotions and fears it brought to the surface.

I don't remember much of that day either, but I do remember Sarah suggesting tools would be needed to see me through this. Tools? I hadn't heard that term before, but it simplified things for me. Yet I was skeptical when she suggested yoga, meditation, journaling, and reading—really anything to quiet my brain and turn down the volume on my negative thoughts: "OK," I thought to myself. "I'll do it for my wife, but it won't work . . ."

I'd been dealing with this for fifteen years, and my solution to any problem in life was to run over it. I'm guessing that most men feel this is the right approach, but with Sarah's guidance, I learned nothing could be further from the truth.

I was at the point where I literally couldn't get out of bed, sometimes for days at a time. My self-pity had become debilitating, and all I wanted to do was to be in a dark room, left alone. I had no trouble convincing myself that no one would care if I were gone altogether. Now Sarah wanted me to not only come out of my room, but try something completely unfamiliar.

My wife's cousin Dani is a yoga instructor and lived with us at the time, and she encouraged me to attend her yoga classes. That way I could take Sarah's advice to try yoga, but be with a familiar face, which would hopefully reduce my anxiety about attending my first practice. Although this did help, I still approached yoga as a joke, and I attended merely to appease Sarah and Corey.

At the end of each yoga session, participants lie on the ground (a pose known as Shavasana) and meditate/deep breathe/focus on thoughts of gratitude. While lying there at the end of my first session, my skeptical inside voice was saying, "This body-and-soul mumbo jumbo is never gonna work." But then, Sarah's encouragement and Corey's insistence entered my mind, pushing out my negative thoughts. Lo and behold, three minutes later, my headache, irritability, and anxiety were gone.

Of course, I immediately noticed the absence of my headache, because I didn't know life without one. Was it just a coincidence? Normally I would go weeks at a time before having a momentary respite from the incessant pain.

Regardless, I stayed headache-free for close to an hour. I was shocked.

I continued with Sarah's yoga experiment, even though I wasn't great at yoga. Truth be told, at my second session the competitor in me was looking forward to debunking the results from the previous day, but instead I once again found peace within Shavasana. This time the relief lasted for more than two hours. Imagine experiencing a headache 360 days a year for fifteen years and suddenly having peace two days in a row! Each time, the calm in my head was extended, and it encouraged me to explore more about spirituality and yoga. Ultimately, I purchased a yoga membership.

Sarah was thrilled and felt it was time to introduce another tool: books on Buddhism. Sarah's counseling sessions are spiritual: not religious, but with a peaceful Buddhism influence. She suggested I read *The Art of Happiness* by the Dalai Lama. It was a game changer.

My toolbox of yoga, meditation, reading, and journaling was taking me down a positive path. With continued effort and Sarah's guidance, I no longer felt helpless. Looking back, I realize she gave me the strongest and most powerful tool anyone could imagine: hope.

For me, there is no cure. I simply choose a continuous determination toward happiness and wellness. Some of us need only one tool to recover, and some need more. I needed not only counseling, yoga, and meditation, but also music therapy (classical), essential oils, and gardening. To this day, if I don't enjoy classical music, yoga, meditation, and a steam shower with essential oils, my symptoms creep back in.

I've shared my concerns with Sarah about this, and she told me it was a gift—one that shows me what I've accomplished and don't want to live with again.

But really, Sarah was my gift.

—Gary Plummer
San Francisco 49ers, retired
Super Bowl XXIX
March 2020

INTRODUCTION

> *Growth is painful. Change is painful. But nothing is as painful as staying stuck.*
>
> —*Mandy Hale*

What Do You Want?

Nothing is more powerful and affirming than a positive, healthy relationship. And nothing is worse than the pain when a once-healthy relationship starts to fall apart. When we're hurting, when we feel stuck, what do we do? Where do we look when we start to ask ourselves that age-old question: *Do I stay or do I go*?

Maybe you've just found out that your spouse has been sleeping with someone else, and you're devastated. You're so enraged that you could bash your spouse's car with a golf club. At the same time, you're so deeply hurt that you want to crawl in bed and die. You want to hurt your spouse as much as he hurt you, but you also wonder what you did to deserve this.

Or maybe you've been married for more than a decade, but you don't even bother to fight anymore. Arguments just add to the hurt and never resolve anything, and you've decided they are no longer worth the effort. You each live in your own worlds—two people living separate lives.

Maybe you don't know how to ask your partner for what you need, and you hate the vulnerability of admitting a problem exists. Why can't your spouse just understand what you need or see the *you* inside the *we*? Maybe you lie awake at night and ask yourself whether you should stay or go. Maybe you feel like merely roommates, taking care of children and getting all your responsibilities done, but without the passion and intimacy you once shared. Your relationship has become more transactional than relational. You've become a parenting unit instead of a romantic, intimate one. You've forgotten how to prioritize the other person's needs and desires. You've forgotten your own entirely.

In all these cases, you no longer live as a *we*. But you also don't know who you are anymore, or exactly what you need to be happy in your relationship.

Seen and Heard

Everyone wants to feel loved. To feel significant. To be seen. When those needs aren't met, we end up in power struggles without even realizing it. We feel cut off and don't have the intimacy we used to have. We can't come to a happy consensus, because we don't know what we want.

Even if we do, we don't know how to get it in a healthy, honest way.

There are no college classes on relationships. No one teaches us conflict resolution. When problems come up, we feel angry, disappointed, and overwhelmed. Of course we wind up frustrated and resentful! Disappointed, we keep rehashing the same problem with no relief. We end up stuck in a loop. Crushed that someone who used to be so important to us no longer feels that way, we wall ourselves off. We try to make sure we can never get hurt again. That emotional disconnect grows worse and worse, and the pattern starts all over again.

How many of these statements describe your disappointment with your relationship?

- Conflict resolution is hard for me. I don't know how to talk to people.
- I have thought, heard, or said, "I love you, but I'm not *in love with* you anymore."
- I feel cut off from my partner. I even feel disdain for my partner, and it affects the intimacy in our relationship.
- I feel angry, frustrated, disappointed, overwhelmed, and resentful.
- I'm frustrated with the state of our relationship, and I'm deciding whether to stay or go.

- I'm upset about not being heard. My partner doesn't listen, and we no longer come to a happy consensus when we disagree.
- My partner and I fight a lot. This creates immature or acting-out behavior.
- I keep going over the same problem without any relief. I'm stuck in a loop, and I don't know how to break it.
- My perspectives are never validated or understood. I don't feel I can speak up and share my opinion.
- I have an idealized version of what a relationship should look like, and when it doesn't meet that vision, I'm disappointed and upset.
- I'm sad because my needs aren't being met.
- The person who was once the most important person in my world doesn't act like we still share that bond. I don't feel important anymore. There's an emotional disconnect.

These are common problems in relationships, and they can feel insurmountable. But they're not. The pattern *can* be broken.

It's time to get back to yourself, to remember who you are—who your intuition, insight, and choices want you to be. It's time to get back to *me*. When you know yourself, your *me*, you know what you want—and how to get it.

Know Yourself

Happy Me Happy We: Six Steps to Know Yourself So You Know What You Want in a Relationship helps clients understand what they want and how to get it. Often when I ask my clients what they want, they say they don't know. I'm not surprised to hear this. I've been in their shoes, thinking that same way.

Concentrating on yourself develops your *me*. Without a good sense of *me*, you may not be able to find the *we* that best suits you. The world is full of all kinds of people we can love, but not all align well with your *me*.

By using the six steps, you will find your *me*—first, before all else—so you don't jump into finding *we* before you are ready. These steps empower you to understand what you need and go get it.

When you know what you need and want, you won't want to settle. You won't want to partner up so easily or go about it backward. You won't stay in bad situations just because you don't want to be alone, or because grieving the loss of the relationship is too hard.

A healthy relationship *can* be yours. What you need is the intuition to understand what you already know you want, the courage to go after the things you need, and the understanding of your own emotions and those of others so you can talk honestly with your partner.

You need insight into what you think and feel about

information you've discovered. You want clear boundaries and a sense of "groundedness" during difficult conversations. You need to know how to be assertive and put yourself first in a relationship that evolves to nurture both partners. Finally, you need to make strong choices based on who you are and what you want.

This book will teach you how.

I've Been Down This Road

I've based this book on my twenty-five years practicing as a licensed marriage and family therapist and affair-recovery specialist. My speciality is couples who are asking, "Should I stay or should I go?" I'm a results-oriented therapist. I've helped over two thousand couples use innovative and hands-on tools for effective communication and personal relating. That process starts by initiating conversation, expressing thoughts and feelings, and asking what it is they need and want.

I believe that every couple is unique, with its own set of circumstances, and not all therapies apply like they did in the past. That's why I keep abreast with the newest and most effective ways to maintain and repair relationships. I seek out yearly training and education to expand my techniques, and I learn constantly from every couple I help.

I've been married twice, and my second go-round resulted in a healthy, loving marriage of more than twenty years. I have two adult daughters, and we are a happy, blended family. I relate to those who come to me for help, because my first marriage did not end well. I had lost sight of myself completely and faced the hard knowledge that it was time to call it quits. Through my clients and personal experiences, I've learned the power of knowing myself first before creating a relationship with a romantic partner. I understand at my innermost level how knowing what I want leads to the deepest, most satisfying relationships. I've been through it.

That's why, in this book, I provide a lot of self-disclosure about my own past, which makes me feel vulnerable. I share the mistakes I have made, the things I have learned from them, and the success I now enjoy. My transparency about my life has helped my clients through their own processes. When they know I went through similar situations and made it out the other side, they feel encouraged and confident.

One thing I've found in all my cases is that key relationship conflicts stem from one partner not knowing what he or she wants and not knowing how to get it, much less knowing how to ask for it. That realization is the basis of this book.

What to Expect from This Book

Through personal stories, case studies, and hands-on exercises, this book will guide you toward a healthy *me* on your way to a satisfying *we*. You will learn

- to become your individuated and authentic self. The process by which the personalized collective unconscious is brought into consciousness to reveal one's whole personality. The process of becoming self-actualized. When you become more authentic, you get more of what you want out of life, rather than what others want for you.
- to become "differentiated," independent in thinking from the family that raised you and all other relationships you've been in.
- to let go of the negative relationship patterns you probably learned in childhood. When you challenge the parental patterns you've brought to your relationship, you can start to be your own person.
- to provide to your children a clean path for them to grow. The greatest endowment you can give your children is to move into recovery and identify and resolve personal issues. (Wouldn't that be a powerful legacy to leave?)
- to find satisfaction, joy, confidence, pride, connection, and intimacy in your relationship.

- to feel seen and heard, and to be more significant in your loved one's eyes.

A realistic, functional relationship offers all of the above. And that's what you'll have once you read this book and apply its life lessons.

You can choose to read this book in order or jump to the chapters that are the most helpful to your specific relationship needs. In each chapter, we'll look at important behavioral strategies plus specific tools for how you can improve yourself in these areas. Together, we'll lay the groundwork to stabilize your relationship. You can then use the tools you've learned here to:

- talk to your partner about conflict in a way that's grounded, mature, and positive;
- fall back in love by reclaiming intimacy and connection;
- find happiness within yourself, instead of looking for it in other people, the key to avoiding codependency;
- be heard and respected when you voice your opinion, to be assertive and clear about what you want and what you need, so you can come to agreeable compromises;
- break the loop and come at problems from a new angle;

- find a realistic and healthy expectation of your relationship;
- answer the all-consuming question *What do I want?* once and for all;
- answer the other consuming question *Do I stay or do I go?*

Your Heart's Desire

I want you to *know* what you want, so that you can *get* what you want: the amazing, healthy relationship of your heart's desire.

I want you to use this book as a tool to discover yourself, the *me* beyond what your parents, partner, or society has defined you as. The *me* that you always knew yourself to be.

Once you discover your *me*, you will have the mental clarity and emotional reserve necessary to create your most desired relationship, your *we*.

You'll see that when you nurture a happy *me*, you can create a happy *we*. You'll know what you want, and you'll be able to fulfill your dreams for your relationship and life.

Yes, it's possible. Your journey of discovery begins here. What are you waiting for?

Overview

THE ROLES NO LONGER APPLY

"Sometimes it's better to end something and try to start something new than imprison yourself in hoping for the impossible."

—Karen Salmansohn

The Source of Relationship Patterns

Most of us don't know how to "do" relationships. Everything we know about relationships, we learned from our parents. Unfortunately, they also learned about relationships from their parents. It's a deadly trap that's no one's fault. Our parents can't help that their relationship skills—good or bad—and their resulting marriage were passed down from their own parents.

Those of us who are parents realize we all have limited parenting skills. Yes, we do the best we can with what we know, and we try to do better for the next generation. The best legacy we can leave our children are happy memories from the best parts of growing up. But I believe the greatest legacy we can leave our children is our own recovery from past childhood wounds, a halting of the cycle of dysfunction or abuse, so history doesn't repeat itself. Role modeling for our children what is healthy is something to be esteemed, because it helps all future generations.

Because of our backgrounds, we've inherited generations of baggage and dysfunctional relationships. Yet now we have to be in modern marriages without the skill set to manage them successfully. Men and women were expected to accept stereotypical roles historically. But we live in a different world now, where those traditional skills and roles no longer apply. We lack the knowledge we need to be together in our new roles. We're all just trying to figure it out and learn. Some of us take several relationships to do that.

Whatever trouble you're experiencing, whatever challenge you have in your relationship, know that it's not your fault. Everyone in our society is going through this together. A lot of change has occurred, very quickly, and it's caused growing pains. Only in the last one hundred years have women been able to go to work and men to express their feelings. People are learning healthy communication skills and how to have healthy relationships for the first time. It's been a huge shift. No wonder we're all confused!

Of course, family history and societal change are only one part of the puzzle. We all also have to be responsible for our own individual choices. What's so great is that we've never had choices in relationships the way we do now. We can claim this freedom. We just need to be open to learning the skills and cultivating the qualities it takes to have healthy, flourishing relationships.

Red Flags in Relationships

It's easy to say we want a good relationship, that we want a positive relationship. We all want to be happy, of course. Who doesn't? But what does an unhealthy relationship look like? How do you know if you're in one? There are signs indicating bad behavior and red flags that serve as a warning signal and are not meant to be ignored. Have a look at this checklist. If one or more of these applies to you, a problem in your relationship needs fixing.

Signs (red flags) of an unhealthy relationship

- You feel incomplete without your partner.
- You rely on your partner for your happiness.
- You and your partner share too much togetherness.
- You and your partner share too little togetherness.
- You have an inability to establish and maintain friendships with others.

- You and your partner focus on each other's worst qualities.
- You use alcohol and drugs to reduce inhibitions and achieve a false sense of intimacy.
- You and your partner play mind games and manipulate each other.
- You and your partner engage in power struggles, each wanting to "win."
- You and your partner are unwilling to listen.
- Your relationship contains a lot of jealousy.
- Relationship addiction is at play.
- Commitment is lacking.
- You and your partner are unable to express thoughts and feelings.
- You and your partner are unable to ask for what is wanted and needed.

More red flags in relationships

- Lack of communication
- Irresponsible behavior
- Immaturity
- Unpredictability
- Lack of trust

- Infidelity
- Dislike of your partner by significant family and friends
- Controlling behavior
- Insecure feelings within the relationship
- A dark or secretive past
- Nonresolution of past relationships
- A foundation of needing to feel needed
- Abusive behavior

It's important to examine your relationship honestly so that you know if any red flags apply to you. One of the hardest things to do can be simply to acknowledge that your relationship needs help.

If yours does, you are not alone. Far from it. Rest assured, this book will help you recapture the relationship you are hoping for. You'll learn what you need, as well as what you want. You'll learn to manage your emotions and move forward in healthy ways.

This book is for you if:

- you think you got married for the wrong reasons
- you make the statement, "I love you, but I'm not in love with you"

- you want tools to make good decisions about who you want for a partner
- your partner has left you
- your partner has said he or she no longer loves you
- you or your partner has had an affair
- your communication has broken down
- you're unhappy about your marriage, but you're not sure why
- you are asking, "Should I stay or should I go?"

I know the challenges of relationships.

I've lived through them. I learned the hard way that sometimes you don't see the problems until it's too late. I understand the heartache and pain of having your spouse leave you, saying, "I don't think I love you anymore."

I understand, because thirty-two years ago, after nine years of marriage, that's exactly what happened to me.

"I Don't Think I Love You Anymore"

It was 1986, the week before Christmas. I was at the top of my game in life and believed that I had everything I ever wanted: a beautiful house in a classy neighborhood, a Mercedes-Benz, a rock of a diamond ring, and a successful hunk of a husband. Everyone said we were the power couple. I was twenty-nine years old and had just thrown a fantastic thirtieth birthday party for my husband at the InterContinental in downtown San Diego. It was a huge celebration, one of those parties everyone wanted to be at so they could "see and be seen." My husband was elated.

Only a week later, I was Christmas shopping, basking in the holiday spirit of buying presents for the family. That happy day turned into a nightmare and would change the course of the rest of my life. I got to the garage door, my arms full of presents, and found a sticky note on the door. It was covered with my husband's familiar handwriting.

"Please don't be mad," he wrote, "but I can't take it any longer. I've moved out. I need my space. Please don't contact me for a while."

I didn't know what a panic attack felt like until that moment. I raced into the house, checked the closets . . . and to my awful surprise, saw his side of the racks emptied. I was furious and hurt, all at the same time. I went straight to my husband's office to find out what the f*** was going on.

It was raining, and I remember feeling so helpless and scared. Panic set in as I acted out my fear, anxiety, shame, guilt, and abandonment. *What am I supposed to do now?* I wondered. What would this look like to the people we knew? How would it make me look? My obsessive-compulsive self sent me into a tailspin.

As I entered my husband's office building, I tried to maintain a calm appearance, although my entire body shook with anger and fear. I burst through his office door to find his secretary, Sheila, finishing up for the day. I asked her where he was staying, and she said she didn't want to get involved. I scolded her and barked harsh words, but didn't push her for further information, as I didn't want to appear to be the lunatic I felt inside.

Fueled by Vindictiveness

Once inside my husband's office, I ransacked it, looking for any sign as to where he might have gone. I found a message pad with indentations of a phone number on it. I shaded pencil markings across it to make out the number. Fueled by vindictiveness, I called the number. It was a local Marriott Residence Inn. The switchboard operator refused to transfer the call unless I knew my husband's room number. She apologized profusely, but I was livid. I thought the operator was implicitly confirming my husband was there and siding with him by protecting him . . . from *me*.

I dragged my brother down to the Marriott to check the parking lot for my husband's car. He thought it was a terrible idea, but could not stop me. My strong personality was something most of my family members feared. My brother used to tell me I was scary to be around when I was upset. When we couldn't find any sign of my husband at the hotel, I was crushed. I needed to be *doing*, to fix it somehow, but I had nothing left to try.

I kept going over the events of the past few weeks. I

was blindsided, and it was an awful feeling. My brother confronted me by saying that I could be intimidating and that my husband was probably afraid to speak up. He also shared that he knew my husband would have heart palpitations when he heard the garage door opening up when I got home. But I wasn't ready to hear it. I couldn't take responsibility for my part in any of this and kept calling my husband an ungrateful a**hole.

I obsessed about regaining control. During those days, I called my husband at the office constantly.

"You're so controlling," he said. "You don't respect my wishes."

"That's not true!" I argued.

"I need time by myself to think about what I want," he said.

That only made me angrier.

When I wasn't angry, I was consumed with anxiety and depression. It would not be until many months later, when I finally started looking at my part in the problem, that things began to change. I learned that I had to stop concentrating on him and start concentrating on myself and *my* behavior.

Regaining Me

I tell couples who are contemplating a divorce that in the best-case scenario, you reconcile and walk, hand in hand, into the sunset together. In the worst-case scenario, you discover *you* out of the process. It's a win-win situation. Naturally, I didn't buy this at the time. I was too consumed with overwhelming anxiety and depression to think past my codependent tendencies. I had no concept about the appreciation of developing a sense of self, of *me*.

Looking back, I recognize my lack of empathy for my husband was typical. Not once did I think about what the relationship was doing to him. I never asked myself what he must have been feeling to leave the way he did, so secretively. I placed all the blame on him, blinding myself to my own responsibility. I never asked what I did that pushed an otherwise loving person—who had thought the world of me—to do what he did.

During my marriage, I didn't know what it was to feel vulnerable. All my life, I had tried not to express any emotion outwardly except for anger. I didn't want to open myself up to being hurt, taken advantage of, or used. I was the eldest in my family. Growing up, I thought showing parts of me that were soft and nice would make me look weak, like a sissy. Keeping myself protected meant no one could hurt or control me.

As scary and painful as those post-separation days were, they were a poignant part of my differentiation process. I shifted slowly to looking at *me*, instead of simply blaming *we*.

As I healed, I began to regain a sense of myself, separate

from my husband and our relationship. I realized that it was naive to think I had the power to control the way other people thought or felt.

Developing a greater sense of self enabled me to manage the codependent and self-destructive behavior I was experiencing. It all came down to trying to control things that were, and should be, outside of my control. I thought I was some omnipotent being who could influence people's decisions. I thought everyone should feel the same way I did about everything. Even though my intentions were good, my presentation was controlling and undiplomatic.

That realization started a long journey that would eventually lead to my career as a marriage counselor. Along the journey, I learned to trust my intuition. I developed the courage to do what was best for myself, and I gained insight about what I truly wanted. I learned to feel my emotions, which led to a greater sense of groundedness while creating healthy boundaries for myself. These gifts enabled me ultimately to make choices that put *me* first, so that I could be a strong *we* in relationships. By knowing what I wanted, I prepared myself to be a strong partner in a healthy marriage.

My first marriage did not recover, even after a reconciliation that lasted three years and produced our daughter. Hindsight revealed that to get and maintain the relationship I wanted, I had to be expressive and forthcoming by being vulnerable. I did eventually remarry, and despite a fear of vulnerability, I went for it. That was more than twenty years ago. I have enjoyed a wonderful, loving relationship because of it. My husband and I have a daughter together, and he lovingly helped raise my daughter from my previous marriage. They give us much joy.

Second Marriages and More

The lessons that I share in this book helped me through the most difficult passages of my first marriage. They also supported me in making my second marriage a success.

I bucked the trend for second marriages.

The statistics are depressing. According to *Psychology Today*, research shows that in the US, 50 percent of first marriages end in divorce. For second marriages, the divorce rate rises to 67 percent, and for third marriages, it jumps to 74 percent.

Second marriages are challenging for a number of reasons. First, newly divorced people tend to marry on the rebound. Second, once a person discovers that surviving a divorce is possible, he or she is less wary of going through the process again. And third, when a family becomes blended, extra sets of circumstances can create disharmony.

After dating my first husband for seven years, then being married to him for nine, I became part of the 50 percent statistic on first marriages ending in divorce. The marriage had its pros and cons. In the long run, I became too differentiated to want to stay together. First marriages have their advantages, as quite a bit of growth is involved when something that was once desired ends in a process that includes grief and loss.

I work with many couples who experience such a loss. I help them understand that losses are necessary sometimes for you to continue evolving into the person you are becoming. When I became divorced, I had to manage a range of emotions, as I was the one who wanted it.

Guilt was something I anguished over for the longest time. Guilt by definition (per *Merriam-Webster*) is the state of one who has committed an offense, especially consciously, or feelings of deserving blame, especially for imagined offenses or from a sense of inadequacy. In retrospect, I came to understand that guilt was an inappropriate feeling. In practicing self-care, I evolved into a person who, despite a second marriage, is capable of exercising appropriate behavior for the betterment of anyone thought to be a casualty.

We Don't Have the Same Marriages as Our Parents or Grandparents

I was married for the first time in 1982. I was married for the second time in 1998. Relationship tools I utilized then were limited; I acquired them by what was modeled to me by my parents. It was in my own relationships that I learned new rules for marriage and new tools.

As modern marriages continue to undergo a revolution, people want more from their relationships. Women want more emotional closeness than what many men have been raised to give. The lack of relational skills leaves both sexes feeling frustrated and unheard. Tools from the twentieth century are no longer effective in the twenty-first century.

This generation wants to be more than companions. Millennials want to be friends and lovers as well as equal partners. The greatest generation (World War II), your parents or grandparents, lived in a patriarchal society defined by male dominance. Men were the breadwinners and women the caretakers. These unions were formed for the purposes of practicality—meeting the family's basic needs, managing a household, raising children, and securing companionship—in building a life together rather than to fulfill expectations of intimacy, emotional connectedness, sharing, and support. Twentieth-century love falls somewhere between "I like you enough" and "you would make a good wife/mother (or husband/breadwinner)."

In the twenty-first century, however, baby boomers want more of what millennials are requiring in their relationships. Baby boomers no longer adhere to the code of patriarchy. Both sexes are equal, gender roles can be determined as needed, and emotional intimacy is expected. Just as women can choose to become professionals, men can choose to be stay-at-home dads. The heightened awareness and desire for wanting to be more relational is being embraced by all walks of life. Whether straight or part of the LGBTQ community, couples want to feel more loved through emotional connectedness. Even in cultures where emotions are guarded, couples want to feel the devotion they know they are capable of giving and receiving. I find this refreshing and empowering.

New Relationship Skills

With males and females being more thoughtful in developing relationships that incorporate more passion, support, and connection, couples need to acquire new skill sets, tools, and processes to:

- identify and exercise appropriate behavior
- ask for what you and they need and want
- share thoughts and feelings
- show empathy
- validate
- manage emotions rather than act them out
- concentrate on self rather than other
- take responsibility
- have the insight to continually be moving forward

New rules for marriage introduce a totally different way of living. Thriving in a relationship involves asserting your needs and wants while appreciating simultaneously the needs and wants of your partner. Knowing how to do that requires making adjustments to the way you think about relationships in the past—and embracing modern tools of twenty-first-century relationships.

Don't be obsolete. Don't use archaic tools that you learned while growing up and expect to have the intimacy you want.

It's no wonder that two people who come together, full of dreams and positive plans for the future, often lack the skill set to learn to love and communicate with each other. Marriage counseling can help put problems in perspective if you're willing to acknowledge they exist and acquire tools to move forward. Remember, it isn't over until it's over. Even if you're the one who was left, you can salvage a troubled marriage by becoming the person you need to be—the wife or husband your partner needs.

I've learned that most of us don't want someone who *understands* us as much as we want someone who *loves* us. But love doesn't mean having it our way all the time, and that goes both ways.

Start with Yourself

During my first marriage, I was a self-centered *me*, controlling and immature. I acted more like a spoiled little girl than a woman and always wanted to win power struggles—hence the bully-like behavior. I rarely showed my husband trust, and I acted out in hurtful ways when I didn't get my way. It all stemmed from my unresolved personal issues. I took those insecurities out on him and, by doing that, never really developed the intimacy of a healthy relationship.

As much as I was proud of him and appreciated our life together, I never showed him that thankfulness and appreciation. He left me after years of me verbally abusing him . . . and I didn't see it coming! I was totally blindsided.

Whether you exercised bad behavior toward your partner, and he or she understandably decided to leave, or you are the "hurt" party who was cheated on, the process of reconciliation is the same. It isn't about placing blame—it's about identifying what went wrong and how to fix it. Starting with yourself.

Do the necessary work to resolve your personal issues and understand how they contributed to the failure of the relationship. If your partner had an affair, of course it's not your fault that you were cheated on. But be open to the possibility that you played a part in causing some emotions that led to your partner's infidelity. That doesn't make either one of you the bad guy or the good guy. It just makes you both human.

Personal Awareness

So how do you get to this place of personal awareness? It's all about knowing and understanding yourself. Concentrating on yourself enables you to know what you want and what you don't. With that knowledge, you can make good decisions about whom you want as a partner and who you want to be as a partner. Let's explore together, as you create a path to personal happiness and fulfilment that will then resonate into your relationship.

The path to a fulfilling relationship starts with these six steps:

1. **Intuition:** Trust what your gut is telling you through your inner knowing.
2. **Courage:** Have the courage to follow your feelings and do what you know feels right.
3. **Emotions:** Feel your emotions—from vulnerability and hurt to sadness and hope—so you can also feel the love.
4. **Insight:** Look within to know what you want for yourself, so you know what you want in a relationship.
5. **Boundaries and groundedness:** Find stability to manage your inner child's acting-out behavior and other triggers that affect all your relationships.

6. **Choice:** Give yourself options to be able to make wise choices, so that you can attract the right partner who supports your authentic adult self.

Keep in mind that these steps only work if you're dealing with a reasonable person. If your partner is a natural-born jerk, then nothing is going to help, and if that partner has already left you, who would want him or her back anyway? Good riddance! Move on! If your partner has psychological challenges, which is code for "mental illness," that can make developing and maintaining a relationship impossible due to the inability to grasp and understand reality outside a person's own reality.

I always say, identify and exercise appropriate behavior (do the right thing), and you'll get the results you want. Otherwise, suffer the consequences of exercising inappropriate behavior (doing the wrong thing), and be miserable and feel the heartache. This can also be described as accessing your fully functioning adult self, the part of you that is self-aware, responsible, and in control of your behavior. Just because we hit the chronological age of thirty or fifty doesn't mean we act that age when we're upset. We tend to act out by following patterns we set during a much younger stage, often in adolescence or grade school. I refer to these behaviors as adult tantrums—not very attractive and often embarrassing.

When we reach self-actualization (the realization of

knowing ourselves and our potentialities), we can exercise appropriate behavior by responding as our adult self, instead of as our inner child. This helps us continue to grow emotionally, spiritually, and psychologically, not just chronologically. And that lets us engage in mature, honest, and happy grown-up relationships.

In the chapters to come, we delve into each of these qualities, where I share healthy concepts, practices, exercises and tools. I also share stories from people I've worked with. But all cases described in this book are composites. They have been deliberately scrambled to protect my clients' confidentiality and privacy.

By following these six steps, you will come to know yourself and evolve as your authentic self, distinct from the people who raised you or anyone you've been in relationships with. As a result, you'll gain more clarity about what you want in a partner, leading to a healthier relationship. You'll feel heard and seen. You'll experience more joy, happiness, and satisfaction. You'll find yourself with more connection, intimacy, and love, and more of what you want out of life.

Before you become a *we*, you have to know *me*. That process starts by looking deep within yourself to understand what you really want. You have to know yourself in order to know what kind of relationship you need and want. You have to tap into your intuition.

Chapter 1

INTUITION

"Your time is limited, so don't waste it living someone else's life. Don't be trapped by dogma, which is living with the results of other people's thinking. Don't let the noise of others' opinions drown out your own inner voice. And most important, have the courage to follow your heart and intuition."

—Steve Jobs

What Does Your Gut Say?

Your intuition can guide you in knowing what you want, but sometimes it comes up against the powerful force of your desire. What happens when your head says everything is right, but your gut says something's wrong?

Susan was fifty-eight and about to get married for the second time. As a lawyer, she had been trained to pay attention to small details. A week before her wedding, she noticed her fiancé seemed overly interested in his phone. She looked at his text messages and saw a photo of two people having sex.

When Susan confronted her fiancé, he denied doing anything wrong, saying that it was just a wrong number. Even though her intuition told her something was wrong, she chose to believe him. She was happy, in love, and about to get married. She let her desire win out.

A couple of months passed after their wedding, and she couldn't let her intuition go. She knew something was very wrong when she contracted herpes.

While Susan may have gotten it elsewhere, there is a high probability that she contracted herpes from her husband, given that he was her only sexual partner. She could have even contracted it from a partner from years ago, with symptoms lying dormant until the stress of the wedding. Now, granted, according to the World Health Organization, 3.7 billion people under the age of fifty have herpes simplex virus type 1. That's about 67 percent of the global under-fifty population. Some people have the virus and are asymptomatic; some have symptoms that are dormant for years and manifest through stress. Anyone with a history of unprotected sex may fall into that percentage. But for Susan, the evidence pointed to her husband.

Following her gut sense, Susan found more red flags—an unusual number of calls to unidentified numbers at unusual times—in her husband's phone records. She sat him down and confronted him.

Her husband confessed. He had been seeing a series of

escorts and call girls, and he wanted her to consider opening up their marriage. Faced with this proof of her gut feelings, she questioned whether she wanted to risk losing the relationship in order to fix what was broken.

Susan and her husband came to me for affair recovery, and I told her the most important thing she needed to do was to stay faithful to her intuition.

What Is Intuition?

Intuition looks within and tells you, through feelings, what's going on. It enables us to make strong choices that are right for us, not for the other people in our lives. For some, intuition feels like it comes from their heart or their gut instinct. For others, intuition comes from an outside entity, whether that's a spirit guide, higher self, or God. Either way, by following your intuition, you will understand more fully what you want.

The difference between intuition and ruminating on obsessive thoughts is that obsessive thoughts involve ongoing anxiety. Intuition is something you feel right away. It's a feeling specific to situations and people when you need to call upon them.

I'm a firm believer that individuals need to trust their gut instincts, but like Susan, they need the tools to know how to do that. Your gut can tell you something, and you can feel it, but that doesn't necessarily mean you do anything about it.

You need to learn how to tap into your understanding of what it is you're feeling on a gut level. Meditation and journaling can help. You already know what you feel on an unconscious level, but to use your intuition you have to bring that to the conscious mind. You have to be able to articulate that feeling, to say it out loud. Once you do, you'll know what to do next.

The Advantages of Following Intuition

The most important part of a strong and healthy relationship is for you to be a strong and healthy person. By following your intuition, you can understand exactly what you want and how to get it. That's the only path to getting into the right relationship. If you don't know what you want from yourself, how can you know what you want from someone else?

You have to apply your intuition to not just your relationship but every part of your life. Don't ignore the voice of peace within you that's guiding you to identify and exercise appropriate behavior. It's the only way to find what you want, instead of what others want for you.

One client I worked with, Doug, left his marriage after twenty-one years. I asked him what he wanted, and he said he didn't know. After hearing this answer so many times,

I really want to develop a process to determine what it is my clients do want. But Doug's answer wasn't strictly true. After we chatted more, he said that his gut had told him he needed to leave the relationship years ago.

Doug may not have been able to articulate what he wanted, but he knew what he *didn't* want. He knew the relationship wasn't right for him. He was in a sexless marriage, with no affection and a list of unhealthy relationship behaviors. What Doug needed were the tools to reverse that understanding and find out what it was he *did* want.

Your intuition is powerful in warning you against going in the wrong direction. Doug's intuition told him what he didn't want. And that led him to the right path toward what he did want.

Tap Your Intuition

With Susan, who discovered her husband was having affairs with call girls, we worked together so she could trust her intuition more.

She had to be honest with herself about what she really needed from her husband. She also had to be honest about what she desired—namely, not to lose him—and where those two things might be in conflict.

Together, we followed four important steps for Susan to get in touch with her intuition. First, we identified her feeling of betrayal. From there we discovered what she needed from her husband, which was a purely monogamous relationship. Third, we defined what made her happy on her own. Last, we clarified the things she desired that had made her turn a blind eye to her intuition.

These four steps apply to any relationship in crisis.

1. **Identify the feeling.** If you don't identify exactly what it is that you're feeling, or if you know what your intuition is trying to tell you but go against it, you're going to come up against heartache. You'll be at war with your own instincts.

2. **Know what you want.** When it comes to relationships, you have to know what you want before you can explain what you want from your partner. When I work with my clients, I introduce them to my circle diagram. They each define their own desires, and then we create a Venn diagram and see where their desires overlap and where they conflict (see diagram).

3. **Define individual happiness.** In the motion picture *Jerry Maguire*, Jerry says to his wife, Dorothy, "You complete me." I tell my clients that I cringe whenever I hear that phrase or anything like it. That's the last thing people should want. You need to be able to stand alone and be happy, and then

you can figure out how to balance yourself with another person. A relationship shouldn't complete you as much as should enhance you.

4. **Know the difference between intuition and desire**. Having intuition about what is right for you isn't the same as desiring something. You can desire something that's bad for you, and we often do. So how do you know the difference? If you have a good sense of self, your intuition will never guide toward something that's going to hurt you or others. If you feel lust for a person, but your intuition tells you the person is bad news, you have to identify which is which.

Listening to your intuition will help you get to the bottom line of how a decision will make you feel. Are you going to enjoy this in the long term? Or are you making a decision that will be good in the short term but hurt you down the road? Susan ignored her instincts in favor of short-term happiness, but in the end the consequences were clear. If she continues to feel distrust about her marriage and sees more red flags about her husband's philandering behavior, the prognosis will be poor for her long-term happiness.

It's easy to look at your life as a series of quick decisions. This person is attractive, this person looks good on paper, this person makes me laugh. But intuition asks questions:

- How does this person complement me and the things I want in the long term?
- How will this relationship weather changes?
- What will this relationship look like twenty-five years from now?

Your goal is a healthy relationship that will withstand the changes life brings.

Let Intuition Be Your Guide

Your intuition can help you focus on what you want, instead of what you don't want.

When Debra came to me, she was thirty-one years old. She had two children, ages nine and seven, and she was an officer in the Navy. She had learned to be strong, not just because of her line of work, but because of a long life of taking care of others. At just sixteen years of age, she took on the responsibility of caring for both her mother and younger siblings.

Debra became my client because she wanted to process tension between her and her husband, Dan. She was resentful because she felt responsible for the entire household. She wanted help from him, but she couldn't make herself ask for it. In session, I asked her what she wanted from her relationship, and she said she didn't know.

So I asked her, "What does your intuition say?"

She realized that she had never had the opportunity to think about what she wanted, even as a young girl. For her entire life, she had been prioritizing the needs of others above her own. After a life of needing to take on more than her fair share of responsibility, asking for help made her feel weak. Being a naval officer only reinforced the idea that she needed to be independent and lead in order to be strong.

Now her intuition told her that something was wrong in her marriage, but she didn't have the tools to express what that something was. She had never had a healthy relationship that she could draw from. I knew that was where we needed to start. Using my circle diagram tool, we framed what a strong relationship meant to her.

Then I helped her put words to the feelings in her gut. We created a "wants list" and a "moving-forward plan" to define based on what her intuition was telling her, what she wanted, and how she planned to get there. Her intuition had been right all along. She just needed help listening to it.

Healthy Relationship Priorities

Here's what a healthy relationship looks like (as shown in my circle diagram).

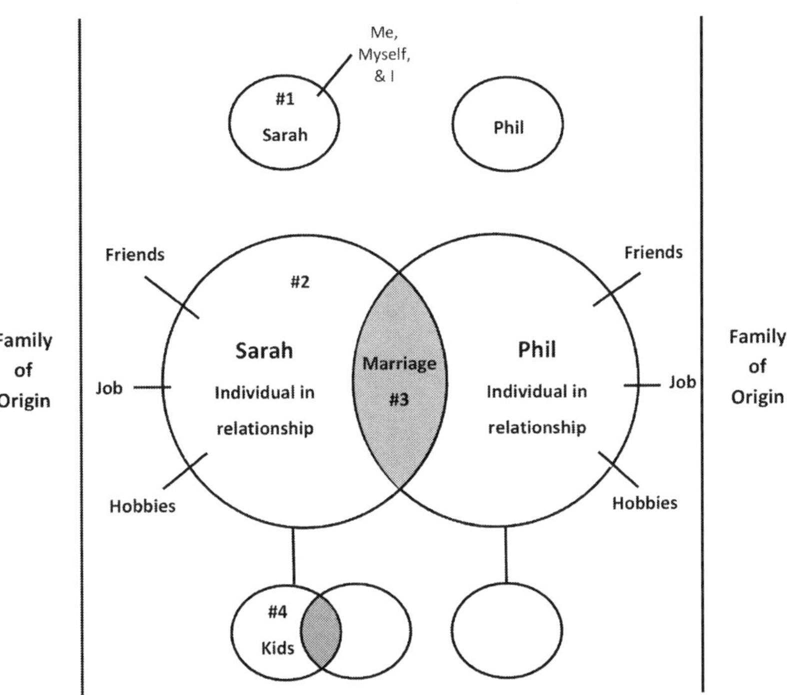

In a healthy relationship, the individual self is the number one priority (me, myself, and I). The individual in the relationship is the number two priority, while the relationship itself is the number three priority. This lets you stay independent in an interdependent relationship. Finally, any children you might have are the number four priority. (See circle diagram)

Some people say their children are their most important priority, putting them in the number one priority slot. This may seem selfless, but it can be damaging to your children in the long term. You need to model a healthy and strong relationship, so they understand and are able to manifest the same with their prospective life partners.

It's like when you're on an airplane, and the flight attendant always tells you that in case of an emergency, put on your own oxygen mask before putting one on your child. You have to take care of yourself before you can take care of others.

Signs You're in an Unhealthy Relationship

An incredibly important part of trusting your intuition is learning to read the signs of an unhealthy relationship. Often, we don't want to trust our intuition because we don't want to admit a problem exists, but ignoring red flags can be detrimental to relationships. A red flag is an intuitive feeling that helps you process your gut reactions to behaviors that are not okay with you. When searching for that special someone, red flags simply cannot be ignored. They'll eventually harm you and your relationship.

A partial list of red flags follows, courtesy of author and

psychiatrist Dr. Abigail Brenner, and including my personal interjections:

1. **Lack of communication.** These individuals find it difficult to talk about issues or express how they feel. When it would seem most important to be open and honest, they tend to distance themselves emotionally. This leaves their partners hanging—or dealing with a situation alone. Often, whatever is communicated is expressed through moodiness and sometimes the dreaded "silent treatment." This can be deemed as passive-aggressive (being aggressive in passive ways to avoid looking like the bad guy) and/or "read my mind."

2. **Irresponsible, immature, and unpredictable behavior.** Some people have trouble mastering basic life skills—taking care of themselves, managing their finances and personal spaces, holding onto their jobs, and making plans for their lives and futures. Small crises surrounding the way people in this category live their daily lives may take up a lot of time and energy, leaving little time and energy left for you. These people are still working on growing up. In other words, it will be hard to rely on them for anything. In a male, this can look like a "man-boy" or "mama's boy";

for a female, this can look like "daddy's little girl/ princess."

3. **Lack of trust.** A person who has difficulty being honest with himself or herself may find it hard to be honest with you. Some of this behavior isn't calculated and malicious, but simply a learned habit of coping. However, being openly lied to is a no-brainer. A person who stays unaccountable for his actions lacks integrity and respect for his partner. You may feel, and rightly so, that a lot of "missing pieces" occur in your partner's explanations, whether simply unknown or purposely hidden from you. I believe if the words don't add up, it's usually because the truth wasn't included in the equation. Also, if someone says they are going to do something but doesn't, their lack of follow through becomes an integrity issue as well. Too many of these gaps in a relationship create mistrust.

4. **Dislike of your partner by significant family and friends.** If something is "off" about this person that seems obvious to those who know you well, you may need to listen to what they're telling you. Often, when you're in the throes of a new relationship, hearing criticism about your new "beloved" may not be welcome, but others may see things more

clearly from an outsider's perspective. At the very least, hear these people out.

5. **Controlling behavior.** Similarly, a partner may attempt to "divide and conquer," driving a wedge between you and other significant people in your life. They may be jealous of your ongoing relationships or simply feel the need to control where you go and who you associate with, limiting your world to allow in only what is important to them. Sometimes, partners like this make you choose them over significant others as an expression of "love."

6. **Feelings of insecurity in the relationship.** You often may feel that you don't know where you stand in a relationship. Rather than moving forward and building on shared experiences that should be strengthening your connection, you feel uncomfortable, uncertain, or anxious about where it's heading. You may seek reassurances from your partner, but these are momentary and fleeting. As a result, you may be working double-duty to keep the relationship on track, while your partner contributes little. When someone in a relationship is doing way too much, I refer to them as overfunctioning. When someone overfunctions, the other tends to underfunction, creating frustration and resentment.

7. **A dark or secretive past.** Behaviors that are suspect, illegal activities, and addictive behaviors that haven't been resolved are obvious red flags. You shouldn't ignore or excuse anything that strikes you as strange or makes you feel uncomfortable. (Of course, if a person has done the necessary corrective work and continues doing so for his or her own good and for the good of the relationship, that's a different story.)

8. **Non-resolution of past relationships.** This includes not just intimate relationships, but those with family members and friends. If a person is unable to evaluate why past relationships haven't worked out, or consistently blames the other party for the problems, you can bet with a great deal of confidence that the same thing could happen with your relationship.

9. **A foundation for the relationship of needing to feel needed.** Often, we enter into a relationship strongly identified with our needs. Perhaps you must do certain things for your partner to make him or her feel secure and satisfied, or you allow your partner to feel needed by fulfilling your needs. If this dynamic is the focal point of a relationship, however, there may be little room for real growth, individually or as a couple, as the partners are codependent.

10. **Abusive behavior.** Finally, of course, any form of abuse, from the seemingly mild to the overtly obvious—verbal, emotional, psychological, and certainly physical—is not just a red flag, but a huge banner telling you to get the hell out immediately and never look back.

Using your intuition is the best path to a healthy relationship. Understand yourself, then your partner, then how you and your partner fit together.

Your intuition is a powerful guide for what to do. But just because you know what to do, you might still lack the key quality to actually take action: courage.

Chapter 2

COURAGE

"You get in life what you have the courage to ask for."
—Nancy D. Solomon

Courage to Take the Next Step

How far would you go to avoid disapproval?

Tom, one of my clients, was a high-functioning thirty-two-year-old chemist. He had been married for a year, but he hadn't yet found the courage to tell his parents.

A year ago, during an introduction visit, his mother expressed disapproval of his now-wife because she wasn't of their culture or, in his mother's opinion, educated enough. So he got married in secret. His wife was understandably hurt and wanted him to be proud of his marriage.

After I worked with this couple, I asked Tom if he still wanted to be his mommy's little boy or his wife's husband. Tom realized that his fear of losing his mother's approval was holding him back from being the man he wanted to be.

Tom finally mustered his courage and made a phone

call to his parents. His mother was standoffish, but his father offered congratulations. By overcoming his fear of disapproval, Tom's courage grew, and he earned the respect of his parents, his wife, and, most important, himself.

It takes courage to leave what feels familiar and do something different. There absolutely will be discomfort. I say, feel the discomfort. When you find the courage to do the right thing, you move closer to what you want and a happier relationship.

What Does Courage Mean?

Courage is the strength to take actionable steps toward the things that you want. It means asking unequivocally for what you need. Sharing your feelings requires courage, as does being assertive enough to make sure your needs are being met. The process of harnessing your courage is one that you can learn. It's never too late to begin to take charge of your own life and your own happiness.

When you don't have courage, feelings of discomfort and guilt dominate and guide your actions. It's so easy to say, "I don't want anyone to get hurt." That leads people to avoid saying what they need and want, because they don't want the other person to feel bad.

I refer to this as the elephant in the room. Everyone knows an issue needs to be discussed, but they can't or won't do it. They're too afraid of the ramifications of where that conversation is going. This may sound super cheesy, but I say, "Don't ignore the elephant in the room!" because later, when it shits, it creates an even bigger problem than if you had dealt with it in the first place.

With courage, you allow yourself to be vulnerable. You accept temporary pain, for yourself and others, in exchange for happiness on the other side. And you acknowledge that you can't control the pain of others. The person you're with is going to feel certain feelings, and you have to let go of your sense of responsibility for that.

The Courage to Walk Away

Leaving my first husband provided one of my biggest lessons in courage. We met in high school and dated seven years and then were married for nine years. We practically grew up together.

I had come home one day to a sticky note left on the garage door saying he was leaving me. I had then gone on a rampage, looking for him at his office and a hotel. We reconciled for three years and had our child. Not surprisingly, we still ended up divorcing.

In a turn of events, because of bad business dealings, he ended up in prison. He was given a ten-year sentence, of which he served five years. While he was in prison, I was part of his support system. I visited him every week, giving him hope through the long days.

During my visits, I was mindful to be uplifting and conversational. We would talk fondly about our past and reminisce about fun days. Our conversations were better than they had been since the ordeal of his indictment and guilty verdict.

The relationship was already weak, and the addition of his imprisonment didn't help, although we seemed to be getting along fine, and it appeared we were becoming close again. We talked about living a simpler life when he got out, which sounded attractive.

During our marriage, we were ambitious people who, despite our already fortunate and luxurious lifestyle, wanted bigger and better. We bought a two-acre piece of land in a high-end community to build a showcase of a home, and we made plans to take his business national. Success comes with a price, and those sacrifices were becoming evident.

One day, as I sat across him at the prison, he said, "Why don't we get married again?"

I was shocked beyond belief.

Then he asked again. "Will you marry me?"

I thought I had put this hard subject to rest, as his legal problems had contributed to the dissolution of our marriage. I stuttered, unsure of what to say. I didn't want to hurt him. He was already in a weak position being in prison. To say anything other than yes seemed like a kick in the teeth. He was at his lowest point in life. But to say yes would have continued the inauthenticity. That answer would meet his needs, not mine. I was so afraid to say my truth.

After everything he had done for me, I wanted to take care of him. I didn't want to say no. I didn't want to hurt him again. Besides, we had so much history together, our families got along well, and, of course, we had our precious daughter together.

With what we both went through, and the lessons learned from the past few years, I thought we had what it took to manage any situation for moving forward.

I fooled myself into thinking it could get better. I had a fantasy of a great marriage. But all along, my intuition said, "I can't stay with this person. I love him, but I'm not *in* love with him."

I looked at him and nodded my head. "Yeah. That would be great."

Suddenly, everything seemed surreal. My blood pressure rose, and my face got hot. I was surprised how I held it together long enough to take a Polaroid picture to commemorate the day. It was a new engagement day for us. He gave me the photo to take home and share with my parents and our daughter.

I immediately sunk back into my codependent self and wanted to cry. My anxiety was off the charts during the two-hour drive home from the prison. The silence in the car gave me the opportunity to assess my reasons for not wanting to remarry—and the dishonest answer I had given him—and helped me manage my feelings, which again included guilt.

"I'm not doing anything wrong if I don't want to remarry," I said to myself. "I want to restart my life as a differentiated individual."

Differentiation is the ability to be in emotional contact with others yet still be autonomous in one's own emotional functioning. Because he and I were enmeshed (undifferentiated), I wasn't able to be *me* and all that comes with growing up emotionally.

As grueling as that drive home was, I was able to take myself off the hook and put things in perspective. *My* perspective.

All that week, I suffered from major anxiety. I couldn't eat or sleep. I agonized when sharing all this with my parents. They were in favor of the engagement. I believe I even told my five-year-old daughter this might happen. She was elated, and I felt like an even bigger fool. Finally, I accepted what I had known all along. It was incredibly hard, but it gave me peace.

The following week, back at the prison, I cried when I told him the truth.

"I know I said it would be great to remarry, but I said that to make you happy."

His face fell. He told me he needed me to be there for him to get through all this.

"How can you ask me to be there for you when I was

never here for myself? I can't marry you again," I said, still crying. I started listing lame reasons. Finally, I broke down and said my truth. "I don't feel the intimacy I need to feel with you." That's when I had to make the "I love you, but I'm not in love with you" statement. Emphasizing the "I'm not *in love* with you" piece felt like I was drowning in a sea of all the scary emotions I was trying not to feel as that codependent woman I wanted to stop being.

I had to buckle up and muster the courage I knew I had in me. I stopped talking and let him speak—not easy for a talker like me. Contributing to our past problems was the fact that I tend to overfunction in relationships, concentrating on other people and managing their emotions rather than my own. My silence was agonizing. *Say something!* my mind pleaded.

His head lowered, and his shoulders slumped. With tears in his eyes, in a sad voice, he said, "I kind of thought as much."

I could feel his hurt so clearly. I had sympathy for him, but I had to remind myself I had done nothing wrong. I had to let go of my guilt.

Guilt is actually an inappropriate feeling. It's what you feel when you've done something wrong. Not wanting what he wanted was not wrong. I had to understand that staying would have been more painful in the long term. Staying would prevent someone else from entering his life, someone to whom he could become the moon and stars.

Leaving would allow room for him to find someone who would love him the way he loved me. But more important, staying would defeat my process of individuation and differentiation from him.

When I embraced courage, I felt happy and relieved. I felt proud because I was able to assert myself. I knew what I wanted for the first time in my life, and I said no.

Your life might depend on you saying no. It takes tremendous courage. But the rewards are the freedom to get what you truly want.

Where Does Fear Come From?

Courage is acting even in the presence of fear. But where does fear come from?

Fear comes from many different places. Societal pressure, family pressure, and cultural expectations can be overwhelming. It's hard to fight that fear. You're afraid of judgment and criticism, so you make decisions that prioritize other people's happiness over your own.

The fear that holds us back from taking care of ourselves is often a fear we learn of being considered self-centered or selfish. Sometimes it can be hard to understand the difference between self-awareness and selfishness.

As a marriage and family therapist, I see individuals with many different problems. One young woman came in because she had a panic attack. She had been experiencing anxiety for several months, centered around her relationship with her parents. They wanted her to give them $3,000 to pay their property taxes. They had money of their own, but they wanted to buy a brand-new luxury car and couldn't afford both.

My client was only twenty-seven years old and employed in a job she enjoyed. But her parents didn't need the money; they wanted it. Once she understood how to develop a sense of self, she drummed up the courage to stand up for herself. She told her parents she wouldn't be able to give them the money, because she was building a life of her own. She was afraid they would stop loving her.

In the past, she would have given in to their requests as a means of managing her anxiety. But any peace was short-lived, because she always continued to have panic attacks. This submissiveness interfered with all aspects of her life. She was nervous at work, and coworkers considered her unfriendly.

But she found the courage to fight that fear. In the end, as much as they didn't like the answer, her parents eventually appreciated the reason for it. They still infringe upon her boundaries, but she knows where those lines lie. She realized her dream of purchasing a home and getting engaged to a very kind and loving man.

Anxiety is a bitch. Manage it before it gets out of control.

We all allow behavior that we shouldn't in order to spare the feelings of others. Bottom line is, we don't want others to think poorly of us or not like us. This can create anxiety, depression, resentment, frustration, and anger. The most important thing to remember is to be honest and open with your partner about what you need, and how that overlaps with what your partner needs. If you can do that, you can start to reap the benefits of courage.

The Advantage of Having Courage

Fear may lead you to think you're protecting those you love from pain, but fear ends up causing more harm in the long run. This is an important distinction. With fear,

- you will never be authentic
- you'll bring that inauthenticity into your relationship and hurt the people you love
- you'll affect your relationship adversely through resentment and frustration
- you'll intend to make everyone happy, but your unhappiness will bleed into everything you do and everyone around you, hence defeating the purpose
- you'll suffer emotional disconnection and shut yourself off from the people you love

Short-term pain from speaking up is the best way to protect both yourself and the people you love. Feel the discomfort rather than acting it out. Acting-out behavior has some really detrimental ramifications.

Take Jennifer and Joseph. They dated for seven years and were married for seven more. But while Jennifer loved her husband, she was no longer in love with him. She had been concentrating on herself for several years, finding out more about what she liked and wanted. Sharing this self-awareness made no impact on Joseph. Because he did not embrace her newfound awareness, she felt disconnected. She had grown as a person. She knew it was time to leave, but she felt immense guilt knowing that she was the one who had changed.

She wanted to force herself back into who she used to be (her undifferentiated self) to avoid hurting her husband. But doing that was causing them both pain. There was an elephant in the room, and it was her unhappiness. We talked about it in session, and I told her that Joseph had to deal with his own emotions, and she had to deal with hers.

Although it was the right decision, it was sad. And it's important to acknowledge the sadness. You have to let yourself go through that grief and loss. That's where courage comes in: to let yourself be sad and know it's going to be okay.

How to Have Courage

Fear can be daunting to tackle, but acquiring the skills to have courage is possible for everyone. In marriage and couples counseling, I help my clients understand that they need to teach people how to behave around them. And that starts with communication:

- Think about what you want from the other person. What is the goal of the conversation?
- Think about how to phrase that goal. What statements can you use to make your goal clear?
- Initiate conversation. It's up to you to take the first step past your fear. This is where your courage will most come into play.
- Share specific thoughts and feelings that relate back to what you want. Why do you want this? How have you been feeling, and how do you want to feel?
- Ask for what you need with clear, precise language.

Once you've committed to communication, the next step is to make sure the other person hears you. This can be intimidating, especially if you've established a negative pattern of communication. If the person you're trying to talk to is used to encountering no resistance, you'll need to make sure you're very assertive when you communicate:

Know what you want (help around the house, for

example). Ask for it: “I want help with the household chores.”

Know what you don’t want (excuses why your partner can’t help, for example).

Use “I” statements: “I would like you to help me with chores around the house.”

Own your thoughts and feelings (anxiety, fear, frustration, etc.).

Make your requests clear. Use “I” statements.

Respect yourself, and others will respect you too. What a concept!

At the end of the day, having courage is about embracing your sense of self and not allowing anyone to take that away. Feel your own feelings, assert yourself, and don’t be persuaded to do what you don’t want to do. With courage, you know what you want, and you’re ready to go and get it.

Once you’ve combined your intuition with the courage to accept what it’s telling you, it’s time to tap into your emotions. Emotions are incredibly powerful, and without an understanding of what both you and your partner are feeling, you’ll end up causing unnecessary pain as you search for your own truth.

Chapter 3

EMOTIONS

"Your intellect may be confused, but your emotions will never lie to you."

—Roger Ebert

Understanding Emotions

When someone asks you, "How do you feel about that?" do you answer with a thought rather than an actual feeling?

I worked with a young woman who contemplated leaving an emotionally abusive relationship. I asked her how she felt about her husband's recent criticism of her. She answered, "I think he had a bad day and took it out on me."

I clarified that I wanted to know how it made her feel, not why she thought it happened. She admitted that she was angry. That was a good start, but anger is a typical reaction to someone's bad behavior. I wanted her to find the underlying feelings associated with that anger. She thought about it, and she said, "Hurt and disappointment. Who says those things to a person they love?"

We've seen how intuition helps you acknowledge your feelings, but it's also important to identify those feelings properly. Most people's first response is to engage in intellectual thoughts instead of emotions. To know what you're feeling at any given time and share it requires vulnerability. Sharing feelings is risky. Risk-taking makes you vulnerable. Vulnerability brings about intimacy.

I grew up thinking, *I'm not going to be vulnerable. I'm not going to say I'm hurt. I'm not going to look weak.* During my first marriage, I never even called my husband by his first name. I used a nickname I made up with the excuse of it being cute and endearing, which it was, but that actually helped me disconnect emotionally. I thought that was a good thing. Wrong!

I thought it made me tough, safe. But it also made it impossible to nurture closeness with my husband. That emotional disconnect created a lack of intimacy that, in hindsight, made it impossible for me to be intimate with him.

As much as I cared about him and thought he was intelligent and objectively attractive, I didn't feel that sense of emotional connectedness. I did not feel those butterflies in my stomach. We made good business partners and achieved mutual goals together and shared those happy moments. He was funny and made me laugh. But in the end, I didn't feel the intimacy needed to sustain a romantic relationship.

With every relationship, we learn more and more about our emotions. For that I am grateful.

When I don't express thoughts and feelings with my current husband, I end up feeling disconnected. Tiny things he does will start to annoy me. But when we're both expressing ourselves, we feel very connected. I feel like a woman who's falling in love all over again, and I get so wrapped up with love for him. It works.

Shared emotions lead to intimacy and connection. If you embrace them, you're going to feel the giddiness that you get from a romantic relationship. And when you have emotional connectedness, physical intimacy follows naturally. The emotional piece triggers the sexual piece, especially for women.

Emotion and Its Significance

Emotions are a key part of making your relationship less of a companionship and more of a loving romantic union. Emotions are what bind you in a relationship. When two people meet, there has to be some kind of feeling, something that elevates it from a friendship to something romantic.

When you tell your partner, "When you did that, it made me happy," or "When you did that, it disappointed me," you develop intimacy with that person. My clients who have had emotional affairs often say the affairs started because they couldn't share their feelings with their partners. When they did, they were negatively reinforced or got pushback in the form of judgment or criticism.

They find someone with whom they aren't afraid to be intimate, because they have nothing to lose. But that intimacy then turns something casual into something serious. They start to have feelings for their new love interest, because with this new person they have a connection. The words *sad, hurt, happy, disappointed* are suddenly being included in their discussions, making their infatuation for one another seem real.

Having emotions and sharing them is an important part of the intimacy-building process. But sometimes the underlying emotions are not shared because we fear being vulnerable.

I've seen this with many of my clients.

Troy and Tiffany, a young married couple in their thirties, told me they felt like roommates rather than spouses. They came to see me because they wanted to recapture the spark. I asked them what being roommates felt like. Tiffany said, "We get along, and we never fight, but we don't feel the intimacy. We've lost the emotional connection." I asked them how they express to each other what that felt like, and they said they didn't.

When we explored more, we found that Tiffany is always doing the talking. Troy seldom shares any feelings, seldom initiates. When Tiffany initiates a conversation,

Troy gives yes-and-no answers. Or he answers in thoughts, not feelings.

Here's a typical conversation:

"How was your day?" asks Tiffany.

"Stressful," says Troy.

"How did you feel about it?" says Tiffany.

"It was a busy day, with lots to do," says Troy.

I shared that a phrase that expresses feelings would be something like, "I had a busy day. I felt a lot of stress and anxiety, and I'm tired now."

Tiffany might ask Troy how he feels about things, but his answer will be a thought, not a feeling.

The solution was clear.

In order to have that intimate feeling, they needed to show each other their most vulnerable selves. They needed to express how they were feeling even if it was scary. They thought it was good that they never fought, but of course it wasn't. They were never sharing any true emotions. Hence, they couldn't feel a connection.

Of course, it's natural to cover your real emotions. I used to do that and sometimes still do.

On one of my milestone birthdays, I had an expectation that my daughters would do something out of the ordinary for me. All my life, I made sure people I cared about felt special. For example, Mother's Day tends to be "another day in the life," as I usually make the plans. My family follows through graciously, which makes for a nice day. I halfway hope they will someday get together and do something for me to mark the occasion.

My two daughters reside in different parts of the country, so for my sixtieth birthday, I once again made plans and arranged my own celebration. They did call/text me to say happy birthday, and I appreciated it. I loved what I ended up doing, but minimized their lack of, in my opinion, placing importance on my birthday. I felt sad and disappointed. I realized I was hurt, but of course I wasn't going to share that with them.

I believe they take for granted that I have wants, because I present myself as quite independent and get whatever it is I want. That's where overfunctioning comes into play. I do everything, making it impossible for others to do anything. Hence, they underfunction, and in this case, I ended up feeling undervalued, as I had set all this up to begin with.

I do understand that not sharing my feelings with my family makes me appear like a hypocrite. I encourage people to share their emotions, ask for what they want, and be vulnerable, but I'm only human and am scared too. Being vulnerable is not a comfortable feeling for me, as you know, so I know it can be difficult for you too.

Whether we're men or women, we tend to hold in our emotions so we won't be vulnerable, so we won't get hurt. But that also stops us from feeling connected.

Vulnerability, as we've discussed, is a key part of intimacy. Without that vulnerability, resentment and frustration grow. When the relationship eventually blows up, it's too late for damage control. It's too late to fix anything, because you've never even acknowledged the problem.

Granted, women and men are wired differently in terms of sharing emotions. You know how women, whenever they go out for a girls' night, come back energized, saying they had so much fun? They spend that time talking, laughing, showing each other empathy, validating thoughts and perspectives. The process makes them feel close to one another, connected.

Men—and this is a huge generalization—will often refuse to open up and be vulnerable by sharing emotions. They talk about sports, work, and other superficial topics. And that's why guys don't feel as close to their guy friends as women feel to their female friends. Again, this is just my perspective, but I've seen it generally to be true.

In a marriage, you want to feel a close connection with your spouse, not just with your friends. And the way to do that is through emotional connectedness. When you start to share with your partner how you feel about something, good or bad, you're going to feel closer to him or her. If you're scared to share, that's okay. That's normal. It takes time to learn how to communicate in a safe, vulnerable way.

How to Deal with Your Emotions

Emotions can also be explosive. There can be anger, judgment, frustration. In the beginning of a relationship, you're feeling the positive stuff only, but at some point, it becomes real. Negative emotions *will* come out. We're all entitled to feel what we're going to feel, and it's important to express those emotions. But you have to find a way to express them in an appropriate way.

"I'm angry" is very different from "You're a f****** prick, and I hate your guts!" Adults tend to tell kids in the throes of a tantrum, "Mind your words!" A lot of my work with clients is about taking acting-out behavior and turning it into "feeling words." But when you're in crisis, finding those words can be incredibly difficult.

When I had a miscarriage at twenty weeks, my first husband didn't want to talk about it. I was bedridden for the duration of my pregnancy, experiencing excruciating pain on a daily basis. I bled day and night and couldn't get a good night's rest. My parents came every night to bring dinner and cheer me up. They could see I was in so much pain and felt helpless. I went to the emergency room several times, and the last time is when I lost my baby. With my baby dead in my womb, I waited over eight hours for my doctor to arrive; when he did, he literally put his fingers inside me and pulled the poor little thing out.

You could hear me scream through the hospital hallways.

I learned that my baby died in utero due to a slow abruption of my placenta. Between the bleeding and the abruption, my son was starving of nutrients needed to survive. It was a horrific experience. Who wouldn't want to talk about it to process that nightmare?

We would have had so much to talk about and process if my husband would have made space to do that. He claimed talking about it made him feel sad, and he avoided any conversation about how his silence met his need and not mine. I was a big-time talker, and that was the way I needed to process my grief.

But he didn't want to talk about it, and I never told him how much it hurt me that I couldn't be open with him. It was a huge factor in our loss of intimacy. Many couples who lose children experience grief and loss differently. Some talk about it and become closer, while others do what we did. It reinforced my belief that I had to be tough, and I stopped opening up at all. Negative reinforcement to my already-hesitant risk-taking almost always guarantees I shut down. I didn't have the tools I needed to express how I felt, to express why I needed to talk.

Tools Inventory

Troy and Tiffany, the clients who felt like roommates, also didn't have the tools they needed to express their emotions, so I gave them a tool called the weekly inventory (see diagram).

Weekly Inventory

Say your partner's name ....

- What about this week did you like?
- What about this week did you not like?
- What particular behavior of mine made you happy?
- What particular behavior of mine made you sad?
- What particular behavior of mine hurt your feelings?
- What particular behavior of mine disappointed you?
- What particular behavior of mine caused you any anxiety?
- What can I do for you this week to make you happy?
- Anything I can do for you this week to help you out?
- Is there anything you would like for me to stop doing?
- What can I do to make you feel more loved?
- What can I do to make you more interested in me?
- Any feedback about our interaction from the past week?
- Any situation/issue you want to bring up at this time to talk about?

I want to thank you for ______________________________

I appreciate that you ________________________________

To use the weekly inventory, a couple sits down together every week for a question-and-answer session. One partner starts by asking a question, and the other answers. They don't switch roles until the partner has asked all of his or her questions and receives all the answers, taking no more than fifteen minutes. Then the two trade places, taking another fifteen minutes for the second partner to ask questions and receive answers.

It's preferable to do the weekly inventory on the same day and at the same time so the couple can develop momentum and remain on the same page. The exercise shouldn't take more than thirty minutes altogether.

To end the session, the couple will thank each other, offer appreciation, and allow some time for any needed clarity.

As you can see, the tool has questions like, "What particular behavior of mine created anxiety for you?" and "What particular behavior of mine disappointed you?" This allows you to pick apart different emotions and see where they're coming from and what you can do to improve the situation. Normally, no one asks, "What can I do to make you feel more loved?" But my tool makes you ask exactly that.

Tiffany and Troy took the weekly inventory home and did it for two weeks. When they came back, they told me they had more positive feelings about the relationship than they had had in years. Troy particularly liked it because it was structured, and that helped him to feel safe about opening up. A lot of my engineer clients appreciate the structure.

When couples become emotionally distant, they tend to talk in single sentence answers. For example,

Wife: "How was your day?"
Husband: "Not so good."
Wife: "Mm-hmm."
Husband: "I had a lot of fires to put out."
Wife: "Me too."

I show couples how to respond with more empathy, which creates more connection. One tool I teach in marriage counseling is a three-step process I call REV. This tool helps stabilize acting-out behavior to continue a conversation productively. REV (or, as I say in therapy, REV it up!) reduces defensiveness with connection to allow space for a healthy resolution.

REV creates an emotional connectedness needed for intimacy when having normal conversations. The three steps are as follows:

1. Do **R**eflective listening
2. Show **E**mpathy
3. **V**alidate

Here's an example of REV in action:

Wife: "Honey, I need to talk to you about something that happened at the dinner party last night. And I need you to be nonjudgmental, hear me out, and not get upset. When I shared a story with our friends, you cut me off a couple of times. You even finished the story for me! I felt disrespected and a bit perturbed."

Husband responds with the three REV steps:

R = "So I'm hearing you say I cut you off a couple times while you were telling a story last night. And I even finished it for you, making you feel disrespected and upset."

E = "I can imagine you feeling disrespected and upset."

V = "You're right. I did finish your story."

Wife: "Thank you for using the REV tool. I appreciate you validating my perspective."

Then the husband provides his perspective:

Husband: "I liked the story so much I wanted to hurry along the cool ending. I'm sorry. I'll keep my mouth shut in the future when you're telling a story."

The process of using REV makes conflict easier to discuss. Showing empathy for feelings and validating each other's perspective keeps conversation neutral enough to come to a resolution and deescalates potential volatility. Using REV in conversations, with no conflict present, makes for a feeling of being heard and seen, which leads to a connectedness otherwise not developed. In other words, REV can make all the difference between staying calm and collected and starting WWIII.

Other tools exist that you can use to help manage and identify your emotions include:

- Stop and sense what you're feeling. What is your gut telling you?
- Feel your feelings. Say them out loud.
- Manage your feelings to help guide you to do what is good for you, not what is good for the other people in your life. You can do this in three ways: take deep breaths; take timeouts; and journal.
- If they are good feelings, embrace them. If they're not, let yourself feel and acknowledge the discomfort.
- Externalize and express your feelings. Doing so ensures they don't blow up later and gives your functioning adult self the opportunity to react in appropriate ways. Don't internalize.

- Don't worry about how others are feeling. You can't make them feel a feeling. They are responsible for their own emotions.

Embrace the Discomfort

Not all feelings are good, but all feelings are valid, and avoiding discomfort won't help you grow.

In the case of Debra and Dan, the couple mentioned in Chapter 1, Debra resented Dan for not helping more in the household. She wanted to ask her husband to shoulder more responsibilities at home. As we continued on her journey, she admitted that she felt resentment toward her husband for not knowing that she needed his help. She didn't want to have to ask for help, because asking made her feel vulnerable. But she came to understand that she couldn't expect him to read her mind either. She needed to face her fear about taking a risk.

It's important to concentrate on your own feelings and not the feelings of others. I reminded Debra that she wasn't responsible for how Dan felt if he didn't like her request. Holding in the burden of her emotions only made her angry and resentful. It's better to ask for what you need and want, so your partner has the opportunity to give it . . . or not. Either way, you'll know, and you'll be able to move forward with honesty and intimacy.

You know the truth by the way it feels. In connecting to your emotions, you connect to the truth at the heart of everything you do and experience. When you follow that truth, it will lead you to real and powerful insight.

Chapter 4

INSIGHT

"A moment's insight is sometimes worth a life's experience."

—Oliver Wendell Holmes, Sr.

Constant Flirting

A couple came to me because the husband flirted constantly—with waitresses, bartenders, salespersons, everyone. He even went out of his way to run an errand for a waitress at their favorite restaurant, helping her pick up furniture and delivering it to her home.

His wife told him this hurt her feelings and made her feel like she wasn't being prioritized. She said it was being unfaithful, and he disagreed. It's not like he was having an affair, after all.

As they talked it out, I asked him why he engaged in this behavior. He said that after fifteen years and three kids, he and his wife were wrapped up in the day-to-day details of life. Their conversations felt transactional rather than emotional and intimate. Flirting was superficial, but it made him feel important, significant.

That was his moment of insight.

He realized that what he chased was that feeling. He loved his wife, and he wanted that feeling from her. If he got it, he would have little need to flirt with other women.

Now, when he promised not to flirt with others, his wife believed him. She had the insight that she could help nurture their connection, which made her feel more safe and secure. In the end, they both got what they wanted because they had the insight to make changes.

Information Gathering

Insight allows you to engage in heartfelt reflection.

Insight helps you understand what's going on in your relationship at any given time, whether you're in conflict or things are going well. It gives you a strong understanding of what's going on with you and how that contributes to the state of your relationship in general. Insight means you realize what you could be contributing, what your perspective is, and, most important, how you feel about that. When you trust your ability to process information (understand what's going on), you learn to say the things that you need to say, despite the possible ramifications.

Information gathering is an important tool in every relationship. The best way for you to gather information is through understanding what you are thinking and feeling and whatever you are trying to process. When you take in information, your brain processes it and provides introspection into what you know and how you feel. Think of insight as an expansion of your personal opinion. It takes the information you've gathered and digests it in a thoughtful, rather than a half-witted, way.

Insight is the ability to gather information, process that information, and finally be able to articulate what that gathered information means to you. An important thing to remember when examining your reaction to information is that want and need are also mixed in there, and it's important to use insight to sort them out. Think of *need* as something you must have to survive, like food; and *want* as a preference, like ice cream.

Insight versus Intuition

When we talk about want or need, we can also use the terms intuition and insight. Insight appeals to the intellectual side of your brain, while intuition is more focused on the gut and the heart. Intuition tells you what you want, but insight collects gathered information and processes it like a computer, showing you what you need.

Insight will feel different for every person. It relies on how you gather information, how you process it, and then how you articulate it. Imagine if you're fighting with your partner about chores. Your partner might say, "I left the dirty cup there because I planned to wash it later, and then I forgot." You might hear that and think, *You don't love me enough to remember a clean kitchen is important to me.*

But when you sit down and have an information-gathering discussion, you'll gain insight into *why* your partner has trouble remembering chores that are important to you. Maybe your partner has just as much trouble remembering things you know are important to them, like remembering when a favorite show comes on. Maybe your partner is overwhelmed by work. Maybe he or she feels ignored and leaves the dishes to provoke a fight. When you get insight from processing that discussion, you'll understand how the problem fits into the situation at hand.

Something that seems like a small problem often is actually an indicator of a greater problem in your relationship. There's one clear indicator that a person is capable of modifying problematic behavior: if the person has insight into why it happened. For example, if a person has cheated, a good prognosis in affair recovery includes the cheater (affair partner) having the insight to understand why he or she went down that bad road and being able to articulate to the hurt partner why it won't happen again.

The big question is: What did the affair mean to the cheater? If you're fighting, what is the root cause of that fight? What is your part in the argument? If you aren't willing to dig deep and see why the behavior is happening, no road forward exists. But if you stop and think about it and use your insight to understand yourself in that particular situation, you have acquired a skill to manage problems that come up in relationships. There's hope.

It really comes down to processing information. You're given new information, you process it, you understand what's happened, and you articulate that for your partner. It helps you both to understand why you engage in certain patterns of behavior.

Self-Focus Is Not Narcissism

When you're concentrating on yourself, you walk a fine line between self-care and narcissism. The difference is that heartfelt reflection doesn't hurt anyone else. Self-care is about awareness, whereas narcissistic behavior is a single-minded focus that can hurt other people.

Narcissism was a huge problem in my first marriage—for me. Although I did love my first husband, I believe I married him because he was a catch. He looked good on paper and provided an elevation to the Caucasian, dominant culture. The fact that he was interested in me made me feel good, made me feel superior. But it was all on the exterior.

Then I started using insight to learn about what I really wanted and needed from a relationship. I realized that all of my decisions about my first marriage were based on notions of what I *wanted*, instead of what I needed. I wanted someone who was in a leadership role. I wasn't going to marry an employee of a company; he had to be the owner or CEO.

My husband gave me everything I thought I wanted, but I always wanted more. I wanted to upgrade my diamond, to own a big house, to have all the luxuries in life. I wanted him to be powerful so I could feel powerful. In hindsight, I was masking the shame of my personal issues. I wanted to stay in the marriage for the wrong reasons.

When I got divorced, I sold that ring and gave him the $10,000 to start a new life when he got out of prison. Insight made me realize I had been greedy. It was like I had stolen that ring, because I had used how much he wanted me to take what I wanted. I had met all of my wants, but none of my needs. My anxiety was through the roof. I knew on some level that I was a fraud.

The way I thought and the way I felt didn't match up. I couldn't escape a feeling of incongruence. I had checked off every box on my "successful relationship" checklist, which was developed through notions from my upbringing and being a socialized female in a patriarchal society. But deep down, I knew it wasn't really what I wanted. It was like I was in survival mode, trying not to live the life my parents lived while in denial about the issues I eventually came to resolve.

I was a fraud because I didn't feel the intimacy that I knew a husband and a wife are supposed to feel. I felt like he was my buddy and partner in business, and he was nice enough. But I wasn't happy. I would create power struggles, getting in his face and telling him what to do. I used to laugh at the idea of a 6-foot, 2-inch white man who looked like the hot actor George Clooney being bossed around by a 5-foot, 2-inch petite Asian girl. I thought, "God, I'm such a bitch."

After I processed the insight, it finally came together. I was with him for stability, but it was making us both unhappy. I needed to be independent. I needed to seek a relationship I was invested in. I needed to leave the comfort and stability of the marriage. I felt the fear of getting what I needed, but I knew I had to make a change. And gaining success every step of the way while making those changes, I felt the confidence that led to the validation I needed to continue.

From Insight to Individuation

Insight is a valuable tool for dealing with specific situations, but it also applies to a much larger aspect of healthy relationships. That's the process of individuation and differentiation. *Individuation* means to develop your individual self by becoming the person you want to be—becoming self-actualized, your authentic self. *Differentiation* is when you become different from the family you grew up in and the other relationships you've been involved with, holding your own ground while in the midst of others holding theirs.

Individuation and differentiation pave the way to a strong sense of self. It's easy to be overwhelmed by your partner's opinion in a relationship. If you don't put boundaries in place, you don't know where you end and the other person begins. How do you know what you feel about anything if you're enmeshed—two people operating as one in the thinking-and-feeling department?

Stop Being a Chameleon: Overcome Codependency

Just be yourself.

Are you a people pleaser? The reality is that most people pleasers aren't happy. Being a people pleaser can be exhausting, and they can become resentful, angry people. Most of us were raised not to be selfish and to help those in need. That's a good thing if you're able to place appropriate boundaries and set good limits. But many people don't know the difference between being helpful and being codependent.

Codependency is the combination of underdeveloped or low self-esteem (dysfunctional boundaries), caring for others inappropriately (invading a boundary), and over-relying on another's response (having poor boundaries), affecting your ability to separate out what you think and feel opposed to what the other person thinks and feels—all happening within a negatively reinforcing loop.

In *Codependency for Dummies*, author Darlene Lancer defines a codependent as someone "who can't function from his or her innate self and instead organizes thinking and behavior around a substance, process, or other person(s)." Thus, all addicts are codependent. Codependents are caring people, and nothing is wrong with nurturing. After all, people are meant to be interdependent, depending on one another in healthy ways. Just a little self-examination, and redirection, may have you on a more fulfilling path.

Codependency often involves putting a lower priority on your own needs while being excessively preoccupied with the needs of others. When you lose your sense of self because you're doing too much for others, you become an angry person. You might even present with depressed symptoms, not to mention physical ailments. You should talk to someone who can help sort out what is healthy behavior in a relationship and what is codependency.

In couples and marriage counseling, I refer to individuals who experience some codependent symptoms as chameleons, because they become whoever they need to be for the person in their present company. I used to think chameleons change color in response to their environment. However, after doing some research, I learned they actually change color based on temperature, light intensity, and mood. In the same way, codependents change to accommodate what they think a person needs, not just who they're with.

Remember Debra, my client who was afraid to ask for what she wanted? She worked through her own process of insight to learn more about herself so she could trust her feelings. She needed the tools to navigate life situations, and that meant understanding herself on a fundamental level. That process of becoming your own person is called differentiation.

For me, differentiation happened in a single moment. The feeling was so powerful it was almost like an epiphany. I had never had so much clarity. It felt wonderful. I wanted to jump out of bed and tell the world. It was like I had a wonderful secret. I knew then that my life had turned for the best, and I was creating the *me* I always wanted to be. By feeling so different from all my past relationships, I finally felt free to be myself. When working with my clients, I share this experience in hopes they too will receive the revelation they are working toward for their more meaningful existence.

After my divorce, I was in a fairly new relationship with a much younger man. We had a very sexually charged but endearing relationship. During one moonlit night, I woke up from a peaceful sleep. I raised myself up and looked at him while he slept. My picture window brought in a nice summer breeze. While gazing in his direction, I felt completely different from him, detached in the best way.

I had never felt that before and tried to identify the feeling. My insight narrowed down the fact that all my life I had felt an unhealthy kind of attachment, first to the family that raised me, and then to my former husband. What did I know about being a separate person who possessed her own thoughts and feelings? That was the feeling, a feeling of being separate. Goodbye to that little girl who so desperately wanted to grow up. Bittersweet tears flowed down my cheeks.

While getting my master's degree in counseling psychology, I became aware of how enmeshed I was with my first husband. Our personal boundaries were permeable and unclear. This often happens at an emotional level, where two people "feel" each other's emotions. In other words, you're not able to identify and feel your feelings, because you're too busy concentrating on the feelings of others. That comes with overfunctioning.

In relationships, when one person overfunctions, the other tends to underfunction. This creates a shitload of problems, because the one overfunctioning becomes angry and resentful and thinks poorly of the one who underfunctions. The one who underfunctions appears and feels like a schmuck in the eyes of the one overfunctioning. It's a lose-lose situation for both.

For my part, I had never lived on my own and didn't know what that kind of independence felt like. As independent as I appeared, I never even put gas or air in my car until being out on my own. "Daddy," or my husband, did that for me. Being out on my own included being responsible for a three-year-old child as a single parent. But lying next to this new love interest, I felt a sense of freedom and empowerment. I was overjoyed because I had found a sense of being different from other. I was my own person, relying on myself, and I knew I could make it through. I liked that feeling.

I had the insight I needed and was ready to face new challenges. To do that successfully, I would need to establish strong personal boundaries that helped mediate my tendency for codependence. To do that, I needed a sense of groundedness.

Chapter 5

BOUNDARIES AND GROUNDEDNESS

> *"Inner peace begins the moment you choose not to allow another person or event to control your emotions."*
>
> —*Pema Chodron*

Lightning and the Rod

When Claire and Charlie fought, Claire often became highly expressive and sometimes acted out, like a dangerous lightning flash. Charlie served as a lightning rod, grounding Claire's energy. Instead of retaliating, Charlie self-soothed by taking deep breaths, communicating his feelings clearly, and taking quick timeouts before returning to the conflict.

One source of the married couple's tension was their conflicting parenting styles. Five-year-old Katie was having trouble transitioning from crib to "big-girl" bed, and three-year-old Davis cried in his crib at bedtime, wanting his mother's attention. Consequently, Claire and Charlie were exhausted and irritable and had no special time together for coupling. With their relationship on a downward spiral, any small power struggle turned into World War III.

Bedtime is a big-time anxiety producer for a lot of families, especially without systems in place for the children. I recommended the couple set limits with the children and for themselves, which would teach them to self-soothe and manage anxiety.

Although Claire knew she needed to enforce the schedule we developed during therapy sessions, she had difficulty following through with the devised plan. Hearing her children crying when she enforced the limits made her feel like a bad mother, so she often resorted to what felt easier. When Charlie pointed out that the easier route met Claire's needs, not the children's, and shared the ramifications of Claire not following the plan, she exploded.

Feeling judged and criticized, Claire lashed out, yelling obscenities at Charlie and telling him that he didn't know how to be a good parent. She shut down and refused any conversation about implementing the plan.

Claire's inner child was getting the best of her, and she was failing to manage those emotions. Understanding this, Charlie stayed grounded rather than engaging in the fight. His behavior helped neutralize what could have become a highly reactive conversation. And because of his calmness, Claire became calmer and less reactive, able to discuss what she wanted. This gave them both the space to come more rationally to a decision that made them both feel heard and understood.

Groundedness and boundaries are your next tools for creating a successful, happy relationship. When you stay centered, you have a clearer vision of what you want and how to achieve it.

Find the Ground beneath Your Feet

Groundedness is about stability. It's about being in your functional adult, rather than the "adaptive child" (aka inner child) who reacts emotionally. Groundedness means that your functional adult is able to be neutral in terms of opinion and perspective when it comes to both yourself and others. That comes from being fair, not critical, having good judgment, and listening calmly to the other side. True groundedness offers stability, equality, and neutrality.

Boundaries also give us stability. While groundedness is about managing our own energy, boundaries are about staying clear of other people's negative or draining energy.

If you make decisions when you're in a grounded and centered place, you're more likely to make decisions that help you get what you want. You'll be driven by calm energy, rather than by fear and uncertainty. Being grounded and having boundaries provide a stable, neutral place in which to think about how to get what you want.

What Is the Inner Child?

I have clients who can't manage their own emotions. They don't know what they're thinking and feeling. Instead, they're simply acting out through unattractive behavior, which makes them look and feel bad.

In the earlier story, when Charlie stayed grounded, Claire was able to also find her sense of groundedness. She did this by tapping into her functional adult self. A functional adult psychologically manages the acting-out feelings of his or her inner child, which typically include behaviors that are rash, ill-mannered, and predominantly in the service of immediate gratification.

We discussed the inner child briefly in the opening chapter. The inner child is who you are from age zero to seventeen years, whose experiences of embarrassment and humiliation get the adult you in trouble. Our inner child still exists within us. Despite our chronological age, the inner child sometimes causes us to revert to a younger emotional age in order to manage life's stressful situations. In essence, we revert to a lower emotional maturity, which can seriously throw our lives off balance.

The inner child often carries and conceals negative childhood experiences, and our adult selves, regardless of how emotionally developed we think we are, frequently need help addressing and resolving childhood traumas, wounds, and abuse.

During those formative years, while in survival mode, we adapted by:

- suppressing our emotions: we weren't allowed to express them because it wasn't safe;
- being overly critical of ourselves and constantly feeling the need to prove our worth;
- seeking ways to escape, such as losing ourselves in imagination and fantasy;
- disconnecting from our thoughts, feelings, memories, and sense of identity;
- "numbing out" by reading or watching television, or through other unhealthy forms of coping (substance abuse, sex, etc.);
- rebelling in order to be seen and heard, and to create and be part of a safe community of like-minded individuals outside our home environment.

In childhood, we often lose the ability to be our true selves. This forces us to meet our basic physical and emotional needs on our own and robs us of the precious opportunity to just be children. The traumas and abuses we experience at a young age within our family of origin, and the wounds they leave, can keep us from behaving like adults during emotionally charged life events. Our younger selves then take over and try to resolve adult issues through the lens of a wounded child.

When you act in a way that's self-sabotaging or detrimental, it's helpful to ask yourself, How old am I feeling right now? If you're feeling emotionally younger than your age, you may be on the path toward identifying the unmet need(s) you're attempting to meet with your current behavior.

Tapping into your functional adult means identifying those feelings and acting with self-compassion.

These skills can be hard to develop, but they're crucial for life in the real world. I often discuss with my clients that we are truly products of our upbringing. Learning to heal our inner child enables us to identify and enact appropriate coping behaviors at the adult level.

Developing Healthy Boundaries

Boundaries—personal lines that define who you are and who you are not—help set healthy limits with your parents, spouses, children, friends, coworkers, and even yourself. Your ability to set boundaries is an invaluable tool that helps you achieve groundedness and gain control of your life. Without them, people can take advantage of you, even unintentionally.

Do you have boundaries? Have you ever found yourself wondering, *Can I set limits and still be a loving person?*

People often focus so much on being loving and giving that they forget their own limitations. But without boundaries, you can feel overwhelmed and out of control. When you put boundaries in place between you and others, it's easier to distinguish between what is your "stuff" and what is theirs. When you have good boundaries, others can't rattle your emotions easily because you know where you end and they begin. That means you are able to see your part in a given situation, as well as theirs. I like telling my couples, as a visual cue, to "stay in your own lane" when being mindful of boundaries.

Types of Boundaries

You can break boundaries into four main areas:

- *Physical* boundaries help you determine who can touch you and under what circumstances.
- *Mental* boundaries give you the freedom to have your own thoughts and opinions.
- *Emotional* boundaries help you deal with your own emotions and disengage from the harmful and manipulative emotions of others.
- *Spiritual* boundaries help you distinguish your will from your Higher Power's and give you the freedom of personal choice.

Defining a boundary doesn't mean telling someone else what to do. It means understanding what is and is not your responsibility.

Having boundaries helps you recognize whether your relationship is healthy. When couples tell each other what to do or how the other person is feeling, that's a boundary issue. When you constantly fight without effective conflict-resolution skills, you have a boundary problem.

Poor boundaries also include not having any boundaries that differentiate you from your significant other. Just like couples who constantly fight, couples who don't ever fight have poor boundaries too. In marriage counseling, when I hear couples say they do everything together, I tell them they probably have boundary issues. When Evan and Evonne came to see me, they stated proudly they do everything together. They have the same interests and the same friends. They both love sports, food, and wine. Yet they came to see me because they don't feel connected, despite their mutual activities. The problem was that they had no boundaries between self and other. They hadn't established a healthy sense of self or separateness.

Enmeshed couples are codependent relationships. Because they have nearly everything in common with one another, this type of a relationship has no room for other relationships or personal growth, hence inhibiting romantic intimacy with each other.

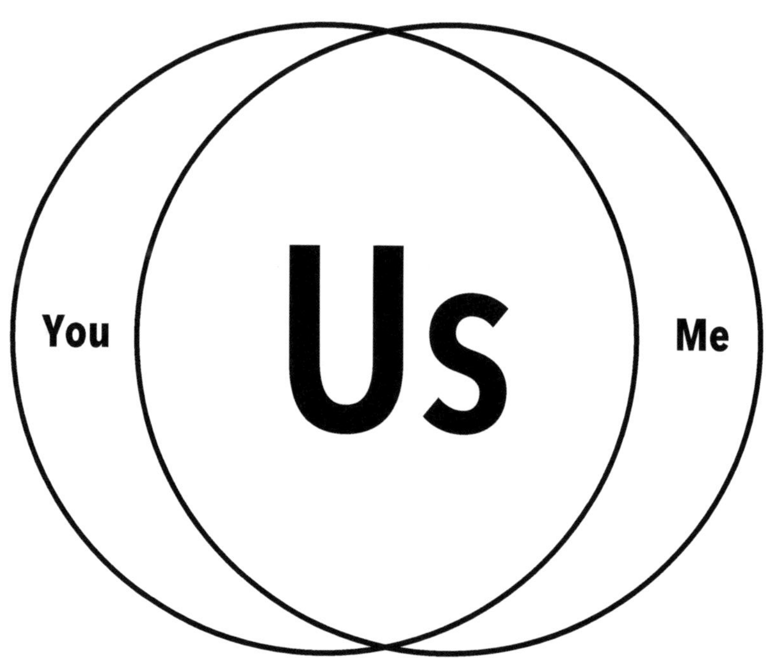

A Sense of Self

Learning to have healthy boundaries is an important part of a stable relationship. It means coming to know ourselves and increasing our awareness of what we stand for. It also means self-acceptance and knowing that we're okay as we are, worthy of good things in life.

When two people with healthy boundaries enter into a

relationship, they encourage wholeness, independence, and a zest for life in each other. Without healthy boundaries, they don't know where one ends and the other starts. Not having boundaries creates enmeshment (Evan and Evonne), and the partners bleed into each other, losing themselves.

We need a sense of self in order to clearly communicate our needs and desires to our partner. Without a clear sense of self, it's difficult to engage in our relationships in a way that functions smoothly and enhances each person. The similarities between two people bring them together, but it's their differences that contribute to the growth, excitement, and mystery of the relationship.

Healthy Relationships Need Clear Boundaries

For a relationship to be healthy, each person must be willing and able to both *say* no and *hear* no. Without that negation, without that occasional rejection, boundaries break down, and one person's problems and values come to dominate the other's. Conflict is not only normal, it's absolutely necessary for the maintenance of a healthy relationship. If two people who are close can't hash out their differences openly and vocally, then the relationship will slowly disintegrate.

Trust is the key ingredient to managing conflict in a healthy way. Look at conflict as a way to gauge the health of your relationship. Healthy love is based on two people acknowledging and addressing their own problems with each other's support. Unhealthy love is based on two people trying to escape their problems through their emotions for each other, using each other as an escape from looking at their own issues. For them, it's easier to project their own stuff onto their partner so they don't look or feel like the bad guy. This is called projection.

Psychological projection is a defense mechanism people employ subconsciously in order to cope with difficult emotions involving placing undesirable feelings onto someone else, rather than admitting to or dealing with the unwanted feelings. Couples do this all the time. An example is a cheating man accusing his wife of having an affair. Another example is a bully taking out his personal issues onto his victim.

The difference between a healthy and an unhealthy relationship is how well each person in the relationship accepts responsibility, and the willingness of each person to both reject and be rejected by their partner.

In healthy relationships, people with strong boundaries take responsibility for their own values and problems. In unhealthy or toxic relationships, both sides exhibit a poor sense of responsibility and an inability to give and/or receive rejection. People in unhealthy relationships will regularly avoid responsibility for their own problems or will take responsibility for their partner's problems. This always comes back to poor boundaries, or, as I often say, "being boundaryless."

Healthy versus Unhealthy Boundaries

Boundaries make it possible for us to separate our own thoughts and feelings from those of others and to take responsibility for what we think, feel, and do. Intact boundaries are flexible. They allow us to get close to others when it's appropriate and to maintain our distance when we might be harmed by getting too close. Good boundaries protect us from abuse and pave the way to achieving true intimacy. They help us take care of ourselves.

Building healthy boundaries requires figuring out what is and is not your responsibility and separating the things you do and don't have control over. Are you familiar with the Serenity Prayer? This prayer is an excellent mantra for learning to define your healthy boundaries.

God, grant me the serenity
to accept the things I cannot change,
the courage to change the things I can,
and the wisdom to know the difference.

Unhealthy boundaries, on the other hand, often emerge from dysfunctional family backgrounds. The needs of parents or other adults in a family are sometimes so overwhelming that the task of raising children is demoted to a secondary role, and dysfunction is the likely result. Consider the role of the father who screams at his children or becomes physically abusive with them as a self-centered way of dealing with his own anger. His needs come first, and the children's needs for safety, respect, and comfort come second.

What children are likely to learn from that situation is that their boundaries, and thus the boundaries of others, don't matter. As they grow up, they may think that if they want to get their way with others, they need to intrude on boundaries, just as their father did. They might grow up with overly fluid boundaries, which can lead to dysfunctional relationships in which they can't set their own healthy boundaries. Conversely, they might seek out rigid and inflexible boundaries as a way to handle their relationships with other people, keeping themselves walled off and protected.

Unhealthy boundaries can look like any of the following:

- feeling incomplete without your partner
- relying on your partner for your happiness
- telling each other what to do and how to feel
- having too much or too little togetherness
- finding yourself unable to establish and maintain friendships with others
- focusing on the worst qualities of your partner
- using alcohol or drugs to reduce inhibitions and achieve a false sense of intimacy

- game playing, unwillingness to listen, and manipulation
- jealousy, relationship addiction, or lack of commitment
- blaming your partner for your own shortcomings
- feeling unable to express what you want
- being unable to let go of a relationship

Without boundaries, a state of chaos emerges. No one in the relationship knows when they're pushing too far or not far enough. This leads to miscommunication and a lack of mutual understanding.

Here are some examples of specific unhealthy boundaries:

- You can't go out with your friends without me. I'm the jealous type, so that would upset me.
- I'd love to take that job in Los Angeles, but my mother would never forgive me for moving so far away.
- I can date you, but let's not tell our parents just yet. They don't know you're from out of town and won't approve.
- Don't wear that dress; I don't like it.
- Don't eat so much. You're putting on weight, and I don't find it attractive.

It's important to keep an eye on unhealthy boundaries, set both by yourself and your partner, in order to establish a strong, healthy relationship. Often, that will mean learning to put your foot down.

Are You Assertive Enough?

Part of having boundaries is stating calmly and rationally what you want, and that means learning to be assertive. When you're assertive, you act confidently. You say, in a direct but respectful way, exactly what you want. At the heart of assertiveness is your ability to know who you are and what you stand for, and then to express these qualities effectively in everyday interactions with other people. Unless they can see who you truly are, underneath it all, other people might not know how you expect to be treated. You have to teach people how to behave around you.

Expressing yourself effectively involves maintaining respect for the rights and feelings of others. It's important to remember that assertiveness *is not* aggression. In many ways, assertiveness is the exact opposite of aggression. Assertion enhances constructive communication and cooperation between people, while aggression shuts it down. And assertion is not manipulation or violence.

Most people are aware, at some level, when they're being manipulated. That leads, for both parties, to distrust and a lack of respect. Manipulation involves hiding behind a facade to meet ego needs. Assertion means tearing down that facade and announcing happily to the world who you truly are.

Learning to be more assertive involves examining several dimensions of your life: self-esteem, communication skills, your ability to remain calm, and your own authenticity. When you can share your authentic self comfortably with the world around you, with integrity and respect for the rights and wholeness of other people, then you're truly asserting yourself. When your best self (your differentiated self) shows up, it makes for a great partner in the relationship you choose to be part of.

Most unassertive people want to avoid conflict because they want to keep the peace. But conflict avoidance creates conflict! Some people would rather have a root canal than confront a potential conflict. Not dealing with the conflict doesn't make it go away, unfortunately. It will actually get worse. It's that elephant in the room again. People who avoid conflict often pay the price, because avoidance usually ends up hurting them.

For example, those who aren't assertive allow their feelings and boundaries to be violated by others. They believe they don't have the right to their own feelings, beliefs, or opinions. And when they speak up, they have difficulty expressing those feelings or needs in a way that's validating. They feel that asserting their thoughts will lead to rejection or even to being attacked. They allow others to make decisions for them and assume that others will care for their needs. They place the needs of others above their own and can easily become entrenched in codependency or victimization by others.

Nonassertive people often feel guilty when they have to say no. As a marriage and family therapist, I tell my clients those feelings of guilt are irrational, because guilt is something you should feel when you've done something wrong. Saying no isn't wrong if it's the appropriate thing to say, and, more important, if it's what you *want* to say.

The ramifications of choosing to be nonassertive are costly. People feel hurt and mistreated when their needs aren't met, but they do little to meet these needs themselves. They may store up negative feelings and then harbor anger and resentment. Their sense of efficacy in the world is diminished, and then they complain about how unfair the world is. This approach leads to depression, poor self-esteem, anxiety, isolation, and anger. Hence, victimhood.

Remember the story about Claire and Charlie? Claire's lack of follow-through continued to create family problems. She kept complaining about how tired she was and how she felt disconnected from Charlie, despite knowing a solution to the problems was available. I brought to her attention she was acting like a victim. What kind of role model is that for her children? She is an intelligent woman, and there is no reason she couldn't get what she wanted.

Despite being able to remain grounded with the help of her husband when it comes to parenting, she and I are taking a look at what could be underlying issues for setting (and adhering to) limits.

You can start embracing a more assertive style with five simple tools:

- Use "I" statements in conversation and during conflict.
- Use facts, not judgments.
- Present your own thoughts and feelings.
- Make clear, direct requests.
- Respect yourself and others.

Develop a Self-Care Plan

The final aspect of being grounded that I want to talk about is self-care. Using self-care tools helps shift the way you think and feel when you're in a funk. Self-care can be extremely challenging for individuals. Taking care of yourself is critical to survival, both as an individual and as a person who is part of a relationship. But it's often neglected in our day-to-day consciousness.

Think of the ramifications of not taking care of yourself as an individual and how that can affect your relationship. A skewed work/life balance, dangerous stress levels, or poor lifestyle choices can all take a toll on your relationship. The breakup rate is high, due in part to lack of self-care.

You can take many small steps to start an effective self-care plan. Begin with a few small actions, then add more as time goes by to ensure that your needs and wants are being met. Learning to apply basic strategies promotes a healthier sense of balance in your relationship. Creating and practicing an effective plan can improve aspects of a couple's relationship and result in a more harmonious and satisfying union. Remember: happy *me* happy *we*.

Essential components of self-care include balance between work and family or personal life, a support network of friends and coworkers, and a relaxed and positive outlook. Following is a list of important self-care regimes in different aspects of your life:

For stressors in your personal life:

- Get regular exercise.
- Sleep at least six hours per night.
- Eat a healthy diet.
- Play with a pet.
- Journal.
- Talk to a therapist.
- Talk to a supportive friend.

- Read.
- Listen to music.
- Dance.
- Get a massage.
- Take long baths.
- Do breathing exercises (take breath from your belly and exhale).
- Practice yoga.
- Meditate.
- Watch a funny show.
- Go outside.
- Regularize your schedule (eat, wake up, and go to bed at the same times).
- Allow yourself an indulgence every now and then (for me, it's a decadent dessert).

For stressors in your work life:

- Clarify your job description.
- Request a transfer if needed or ask for new duties.
- Take some time off. Use your accrued personal time.
- Find humor in situations.

- Take your lunch break.
- Avoid negative people.
- Be more assertive.
- Manage your time better by making to-do lists.
- Stop trying to control things you can't control.
- Express and share your thoughts and feelings.
- Don't take things personally.
- Don't assume.

Another self-care regime for both personal and work life is learning to reframe, a technique used in therapy to help create a different way of looking at a situation, person, or relationship by changing its meaning. Reframing helps with gaining perspective.

Combining these strategies of becoming grounded and assertive and practicing self-care helps lay the foundation to define boundaries and participate in a healthy, successful relationship.

The relationship choices you make should come from a foundation of groundedness and boundaries. Making choices requires insight, courage, and a deep understanding of your emotions and the emotions of others. Choices can be scary, but without them, nothing ever changes.

Chapter 6

CHOICES

"Life is a matter of choices, and every choice you make makes you."

—John C. Maxwell

Hard Choices

Colleen was a wedding planner, and her husband, Ben, was verbally abusive. Incredibly demeaning and shaming, the abuse had escalated throughout the years. Colleen wanted Ben to change his behavior, so they came to me.

In this case, Ben acknowledged his bad behavior. He agreed to work on it, and things seemed to change . . . for about two weeks. Then he was right back to being verbally abusive and volatile.

I wanted to rule out bipolar disorder, as he had some mood swings and could be in bed for days at a time. I recommended a medication evaluation with his primary doctor or with a psychiatrist, but he refused. Some people don't want to know if they have a mental problem or are in denial about it. Mostly they are scared.

Three months went by with no changes. Colleen became depressed, resentful, frustrated, and angry. The years of tolerating Ben's abuse had chipped away at Colleen's sense of self. We talked again in session about what she wanted if she were to stay in the marriage.

With Colleen, I went over the six steps for asking for a behavioral change from your partner.

Six steps for asking for behavioral change

1. State what needs to change, and give your partner the opportunity to make the necessary changes.
2. Give your partner time to demonstrate either an ability or incapability to make those changes.
3. If change is happening, observe for a consistent period of time.
4. If change isn't happening, determine whether a "can't" or "won't" factor is present.
5. If it is a can't factor, find out why, and get the needed help or resources.
6. If it is a won't factor, you may have to leave the relationship.

Colleen waited another three months before returning to therapy. She thought things were getting better, but after their last argument, Ben left the house for forty-eight hours without telling her where he was going. With Ben's lack of follow-through on seeking a diagnosis or taking the anger management classes I had suggested, it was clear that Ben was a "won't," not a "can't."

Like Ben, someone who verbally abuses has his own reality, which stems from his personal issues. His bad behavior has little to do with his partner. His reality is different from his partner's, so until he has the empathy and insight to understand what his behavior means and is doing to his partner and the relationship, it's pretty unlikely anything will change.

I told Colleen that the time had come for her to make a choice. Should she stay or should she go? Colleen had been concentrating on herself the past few months, so she was able to feel her intuition telling her she needed to move on and divorce. She had the courage to listen to it and to face her feelings of fear. Despite her uneasiness, she leaned into the discomfort rather than act it out. She received clarity about her insight as she put boundaries in place to become more grounded. Ben was not accomplishing his behavioral changes, and his lack of effort had created too much heartache for her to remain with him. Now it was time to accept that the only behavior Colleen could control was her own.

It was time to choose. Facing this step and making the decision to leave made Colleen a survivor and no longer a victim. In working on her *me*, Colleen made room in her life to seek a more appropriate *we*. Happy *me* happy *we*.

Learning about Good Choices

When you're growing up, parents rarely tell you to enjoy the moment. They tell you to obey the rules, or you'll get hurt or be in trouble. You must eat healthfully and stay clean, or you'll get sick. You must study hard in school, or you'll end up uneducated and won't find a job. Fear fuels many parents' advice.

Some parents don't allow you choices because they don't yet trust you to make good ones. In addition, they may not have trusted their own limited parenting to help you make good choices. But what we experience as children, and what was role modeled to us by adults, sets us up for the rest of our lives. That's why it's so important to slowly allow children a wider variety of choices, so they are better prepared to make good ones for themselves as they age.

When your parents haven't done that, it leaves you with a lot of behavior to unlearn. You have to take charge and figure out how to make strong choices for yourself.

We all make the mistake, at times, of not wanting to be the one who implements changes. We don't want to rock the boat. We don't want to make the wrong choice. One way to unpack the baggage around choices is to stop thinking about choices as changes, and instead reframe them as possible options. If you give yourself options, you're better able to make an informed decision about yourself.

When it comes to relationships, you're already making a huge choice: to be with your partner. You say, "I choose you and all the good parts of our relationship. I choose you because my insight says we make a good fit." No one is forcing you to make that choice. Unless something changes significantly, you're going to continue to want to be in that relationship, and other choices will all be based on that one big choice.

But a relationship is more than just that single "I choose you." You can zoom in and narrow down to find many other choices you make every day. And each of those decisions affirms your initial choice. Having options makes you feel informed. And an informed choice is one we can feel good about.

When I was growing up, my family made decisions based on what looked good and what the majority of people thought. What often seemed impulsive or hasty was, in hindsight, a lack of information gathering to make an informed decision, sometimes due only to lack of time. Taking the time necessary to make an educated decision took resources and energy that my parents instead devoted to keeping a roof over our heads. Don't get me wrong; when important decisions needed to be made, we found the time to do just that. But in general, we operated by making quick decisions. You can imagine our regret over some of those decisions!

Sometimes I want to make half-assed decisions because

I tend to be impatient or don't want to delay gratification. But my functional adult self overcomes this vice by being grounded enough to know what is needed to avoid bad decisions.

For example, I'm the type of person who wants a lot of options. Whether I'm doing something simple like buying a hat or making a large decision like what car to purchase, I make sure I do a lot of research and extract many options. When I pick a car, I'm not choosing from one of two options. I'm choosing from ten different cars that I've narrowed down to the best three, so I know I have all the information I need. This may appear to be obsessive-compulsive to some, but it works for me.

When I eventually make a decision, I'm confident knowing I made a good one, rather than feeling like I was forced to make a bad decision based on limited options.

Basic Expectations

In my household, when I was growing up, subjects like love, sex, and marriage were definitely not topics to be discussed. Perhaps you had the same experience. My parents were busy making sure we had the basic necessities like food, shelter, clothing, and education. They didn't understand that teaching us about relationships and what to expect in them would help us learn how to be in appropriate and healthy ones.

I am a marriage counselor and mother of two daughters, and it's normal in our home to talk about relationships and what a healthy relationship looks like. Choices need to be informed by a strong backbone of knowledge. You need to know what a healthy relationship is so you can make choices that help guide you into it.

A good relationship should start with and include these basic expectations:

1. **Respect**. A good partner shows respect for you as a person. Although he or she may disagree with you, name-calling or ridicule from a respectful partner is never warranted, even if it's "just teasing." A respectful partner knows and admires your strengths, is gracious about your weaknesses, and doesn't willfully engage in boundary violations.
2. **Affection**. Your partner may express this in words, behavior, or both. Physical affection, such as hugging, kissing, back or foot rubs, or holding hands, is especially important in romantic relationships. Your partner should like you as a person and demonstrate affection in a way that suits your love language.
3. **Compassion**. When you're hurting, you have a right to expect your partner to be there for you unconditionally and with sensitivity. He or she should be tender with you if you're in pain. A partner is not

obligated to read your mind. He or she doesn't have to feel the same way you do. But your partner needs to show empathy.

4. **Intimacy**. Intimacy isn't the same as sex. It means allowing yourself to be known and wanting to really know your partner. More than just knowing whether you're a morning person or a night person, genuine intimacy involves being familiar with each other's emotional, vulnerable selves. Being able to take risks in sharing feelings can be scary, and you might not always get what you ask for. But taking the risk and doing the asking is what's important. The process builds intimacy and helps you become more assertive and confident.
5. **Consideration**. A considerate partner thinks about how his or her behavior affects you. They don't have to give you everything you ask for, or do everything you want them to do, but they owe you the courtesy of considering things from your point of view.
6. **Time.** Every relationship is based on sharing at least some time together. It can't always be helped if your partner has to be away. But if he or she rarely or never has time for you, or consistently rations the time you spend together, you might ask yourself how much more of your own time you're willing to spend being in a relationship with this person.

7. **Interest**. It's reasonable to expect your partner to have a greater interest in you than the average person. At least some of your activities, opinions, thoughts, and feelings should hold his or her interest. A partner who isn't interested in you as a person may be in the relationship just to avoid being alone, and that's not good. Who'd want that?
8. **Generosity**. A truly generous partner enjoys helping, soothing, or finding other ways to benefit you. Such a partner doesn't necessarily give you material gifts or take you on fancy vacations. Giving oneself fully in a relationship is the ultimate gift.

What Do Choices Look Like?

Choices are empowering, both in your general life and within your relationships. That's why it's so important to know *how* to choose as well as *what* to choose, so that the choices you make create better outcomes for you.

The most important thing is to ensure that you have a wide range of choices. This creates a more dynamic life. The same holds true for relationships. Choices make a relationship more dynamic, and the relationship benefits from that.

If you have the ability to choose in your day-to-day, you feel like an active participant in both your relationship and your life. That empowerment leads to satisfaction within the *me*, which leads to a healthy and happy relationship within the *we*. It allows you to stay true to your authentic self.

So how do you make strong choices? Let's take as an example a very specific situation: Your spouse is no longer expressing interest in you as a romantic partner. What choices are available to you?

Option 1: Status quo—do nothing. Sometimes people remain in status quo due to denial, fear, or codependency.

Option 2: Move forward—make an effort to reestablish a connection.

Option 3: Move on—separate or divorce.

All of those choices may not be good, but they're yours to make. We can go deeper, though. Within each of those choices, other specific, individual choices exist. Let's say you decide to reestablish a connection. If you do that, many alternatives could help reach that outcome.

Choices you can make to reestablish connection with your spouse:

- Grow up.
- Stop blaming.
- Become more positive.

- Do more listening and less talking.
- Concentrate on yourself.
- Thank your spouse and show appreciation.
- Stay focused; be decisive.
- Flirt and seduce.
- Don't pursue aggressively.
- Don't be codependent.
- Make yourself attractive.
- Keep yourself healthy and fit.
- Keep your mind and soul positive.
- Exercise this new behavior consistently.

See how many different avenues exist? Each of these is a choice you can make, and each will guide your life to a different outcome. And while you can't control the choices your partner makes, you can choose to do these things for yourself, knowing it will make you happier regardless of the final result.

Let's drill down even further on one of those choices: Concentrate on yourself. What choices can you make to follow through on that larger choice?

- Don't tell your spouse what to do.
- Don't tell your spouse how to feel.

- Establish healthy boundaries.
- Know what it is you think, feel, and want.
- Be assertive enough to get it.

What are the choices in your life you don't even realize you're making? Once you understand the options available and that you're making more choices than you realize, you can be more mindful to choose more deliberately and effectively.

Know When to Say No

I remember my nephew using the phrase "I'm good" whenever anyone asked him if he wanted anything. If he wanted it, he'd say yes. If he didn't, it was his nice way of saying no. Whenever we asked him if he wanted to go somewhere with us, he'd say that same phrase: "I'm good." I came to think of it as code for saying no and not offering up an explanation to evoke any type of feeling but neutrality to the receiver. Smart!

Every time someone comes to you with a demand on your time, you make a choice. Will you say yes, or will you say no? We discussed in chapter 5, "Boundaries and Groundedness," how important it is to be assertive. A huge part of being assertive is making the choice to say no when it's the best thing for you.

It took me years to say no without feeling guilty or thinking I should feel guilty. I had to learn that saying yes to people or situations that aren't healthy means I'm not looking out for my well-being.

I often work with people who won't say what they really want to their partners. They're stopped by fear of hurting the other person's feelings or by the repercussions that can adversely affect their relationships.

If you feel like you're walking on eggshells around your partner, you most likely are not in a healthy relationship. Being able to initiate conversation, express your thoughts and feelings, and ask for what you need and want is what a healthy relationship looks like. Say goodbye to being a people pleaser, and learn how to confidently say no to someone without feeling bad about it. Learning to say no is a process, and it starts when you acknowledge how much a reluctant yes hurts both you and the other person.

I had to face this habit myself. Not long after my divorce, a friend wanted to set me up with her friend Greg. I wasn't interested, because I wasn't ready to date someone new seriously. But I went on the blind date with him anyway, and he was such a dynamic and overwhelming figure I kept seeing him. I kept saying yes when I meant to say no. And early in the relationship, a lot of things were great. He would fly me to his resort and shower me with gifts.

But I started to notice that Greg had a lot of narcissistic personality traits.

Whether we were in Fiji, Bali, or home in San Diego, Greg always had to be in control. He would dictate what time we woke up every morning and what restaurants we ate at. When his teenage son came to stay with me, Greg insisted on telling me how to parent his son—which was ironic, because, according to Greg, I had a role model of a kid whom he admired for being studious and hardworking, and he respected me as a parent. (And by the way, that kid grew up to graduate magna cum laude from a prestigious university and practices as a successful attorney.)

It was easier just to go along with what Greg wanted, but I realized I felt overwhelmed, frustrated, and resentful, and when I brought it up, he reacted very negatively, even punitively. It's interesting how unhealthy relationships appear fine until someone asserts themselves by putting boundaries in place, causing all hell to break loose. Suddenly the person attempting to establish healthy boundaries is labeled as the problem person!

At the same time, I started running half marathons, and that was a great way for me to really get grounded. I started to think about my choices. As much as I wanted to be in a long-term relationship that would lead to marriage, I knew I didn't want to be controlled.

I decided it was time to start making healthier choices. I stopped saying yes when I wanted to say no. I neutralized my own emotions and engaged rationally, and I was able to articulate what I needed and wanted from him. I needed him to show empathy, to validate my perspective, and to take turns making decisions for our relationship. When I started to show a stronger sense of self, he resisted.

When you start to make new and healthier choices, a controlling person thinks you're the problem. Suddenly I had become assertive, sharing what it was I wanted from him. I asked for and requested change, and that tapped into his narcissistic way of thinking. He became defensive, and, not being as reasonable as I needed him to be, he actually broke off the relationship. I believe that, on some level, he knew that he was incapable of being more communicative and that my autonomy would always be a trigger for him to feel inferior and not in control.

Ultimately, my choice to become more assertive and speak my mind led to the demise of the relationship. I could see that it wasn't a good fit for me, despite the benefits—which, by the way, would have been too high a price to pay. I dodged that bullet!

Six Tips to Say No Effectively

Many of us have difficulty saying "no." We tend to be afraid of conflict, as conflict feels uncomfortable. We don't want others to be angry with or critical of us either. As children, we are taught not to go against authority. But we are also pulled by a desire to fit in with and be liked by our peers. So saying "no" would disappoint or hurt someone.

1. Just say it.

Just say no. Don't beat around the bush or offer weak excuses. This only provides an opening for the other person to deflect. Don't delay or stall. Provide a brief explanation if you feel you need to; however, don't feel compelled. The less said, the better. For example, "Sarah, can I borrow one hundred dollars? I'll pay you back in a couple of weeks?" Tapping into my intuition and past history with this person owing me money, I would most likely say no. I would feel bad about it, but I'd let myself feel the discomfort rather than create anxiety in the future when the money isn't repaid. Therefore, my reply would be this: "I have a hard rule about not lending money to friends. I've had issues in the past."

2. Be assertive and courteous.

Stand your ground. You might say, "I'm sorry, I can't right now, but I'll let you know if and when I can." This approach is polite and puts you in a position of power by changing the dynamic. You're taking charge. Another example is, "I appreciate you asking me for help, but I'm stretched too thin right now to devote the time to be of quality help to you."

3. Understand people's tactics.

Many people use manipulation techniques, whether knowingly or not. But don't fall for them. For example, think about when you get a solicitation for a donation to a charity, and the options are forced: "Would you like to donate ten, twenty, or thirty dollars?" Another tactic relies on social pressure: "Most people donate twenty dollars. How much would you like to donate?" Just say calmly, "Nothing at this time."

4. Set boundaries.

People sometimes have a hard time saying no because they haven't taken the time to evaluate their relationships and understand their roles within them. When you truly understand the dynamic at play, you won't feel as worried about the consequences of saying no. You'll realize that your relationship is solid and can withstand your saying no.

5. Put the question back on the person asking.

This is highly effective in a work situation. Let's say a supervisor is asking you to take on several tasks, and it's more than you can handle. You might say, "I'm happy to do X, Y, and Z, but I would need three weeks, rather than two, to do a good job. How would you like me to prioritize them?"

6. Be selfish (in a good way).

Put your needs first. If you prioritize the other person's needs over yours, your productivity will suffer, and resentment will mount. Warren Buffett once said, "The difference between successful people and really successful people is that really successful people say no to almost everything."

As a young woman, I had a hard time saying no. I wanted everyone to like me and, more important, didn't want to feel the anxiety about not being liked. In the long run, though, I became a resentful and angry person. Now people appreciate my forthcoming assertiveness in saying what I need to say:

- When friends request the pleasure of my company, and I'm too tired or decide not to attend, I choose to decline politely. In the past, I would go anyway and feel resentful.
- When I felt manipulated to pay off some hefty student loans, I was really resentful and angry at myself. Now I use my six steps to know what I want, so I make better decisions for myself, regardless of my need to please.
- When my ex-husband brought to my attention yet another pipe dream and wanted $75,000 to invest in this "great venture," and I coughed it up, I felt intense resentment and anger that lasted a couple

> of years. I had to learn to let go of my anger and realized, in hindsight, I should have just said no.

Once you learn how to say no, you also learn how to say yes.

Yes to the things that are good for you.

Yes to the choices that support and inspire you.

And yes to choosing what it is you want for yourself, and from your relationship, so you can live happily into the future.

Chapter 7

YOUR RELATIONSHIP DESTINY

"The biggest challenge in life is being yourself in a world trying to make you like everyone else."

—Anonymous

Relationship of My Dreams

After everything I've been through, after everything I've learned, I can say honestly I have the relationship I want. I have a husband who's loving, kind, and generous. I feel heard and valued in our communications, and he feels content and respected. We're not perfect by any means, but we feel good about our choices in one another. He has his quirks, which can drive me up the wall, and when triggered, I can act out on him, but we agree our relationship works.

We're blessed by two beautiful daughters who are accomplished, independent, responsible, and sensible, who learned the lessons in life I wish I had learned growing up. And of course, I'm in a line of work that doesn't feel like a job, as I have the privilege to help people with their life challenges.

A fulfilling relationship is *your* destiny as well, whether you're still searching for that person, staying with your current partner, or summoning the courage to let go and find the person who *is* right for you.

The key, as I have shown you, is to know yourself first. When you know yourself, you will know what you want in a relationship. By knowing your *me*, you will know your *we*.

With the six steps outlined in this book—intuition, courage, emotions, insight, groundedness and boundaries, and choices—you can achieve and manifest your destiny of a happy, fulfilling relationship.

You can have the life you want and be the person you want to be in it.

You can listen to what your gut is telling you and demonstrate the courage to follow it.

You can feel both the good and bad feelings, despite the uneasiness that comes with sitting with the discomfort, so you don't act them out and consequently hurt yourself.

You can get the insight you need while putting boundaries in place that enable you to be more grounded.

You can make the choice you need to make—and stick to it.

Don't doubt your feelings. I know you're scared, and I get it. Let yourself feel that fear. It won't kill you. Concentrate on yourself as you use the tools you've acquired in reading this book. Understand what it is you want, and go out and get it. Remember it's not what your mother, father, sister, brother, neighbor, or colleague wants. It's what *you* want. And once you know that, you also know what you want from the person you want to grow old with.

Unshackle Old Beliefs

I didn't realize it at the time, but I went through this exact same process. I didn't know what I wanted. I was so stuck being the good daughter, the people pleaser, that I never developed the sense of self I needed to start my journey into adulthood. As you may recall, I was married to my high school sweetheart. I grew up with him. We were together during all of my formative years. Because I was raised to be dependent, rather than independent, I became dependent on him.

Added to the equation was the fact that I am an Asian woman (Filipino American), raised to believe the dominant White American culture was the ideal. My delusional thought process was that my husband was a "good catch" because he was tall, handsome, white, and going places. He had a law degree, and he was a CPA and a real estate broker. His ambition took us places that made me feel valued and important. I knew I had a mind of my own, but I deferred to my husband because that had been what I was taught to do. I was a product of my upbringing.

Little did I know I already had the qualities I needed to make my life what I wanted it to be. I already had what it took to be the happy, successful, accomplished, well-liked person I am today. It's a wonderful feeling. I'm free of anxiety and other self-defeating thoughts and negative feelings. I'm fortunate to have gone through this personal journey and to be able to share my process and clinical knowledge. I want to help you know and get what you want, so your life can be equally rewarding and fulfilling.

Because I have done the work to be the best version of Me, living the best of what life offers gives me endless opportunities to foster even better relationships with those I care about. Family, friends, colleagues, and especially my children and husband. I have a Silky Yorkie, named Riley, who makes my days so happy I forgot what life was like without him. But best of all I have a peace of mind. That is priceless.

Life Is a Moving Sidewalk

Whenever I'm on a moving sidewalk at the airport, I think about it as being a metaphor for life. Whether or not I decide to walk on it, it keeps moving forward. When I'm not in a hurry or I'm tired, I choose to stand in place and enjoy the ride. When I have the energy, I walk along it, hurrying to my destination.

Just like the moving sidewalk, the details of life keep us moving, no matter the circumstances. I think about times when I've experienced major obstacles that debilitated me. I think about other times when I handled a situation well—or not so well. In either case, life kept going.

I hear so many stories of trials and tribulations, and the outcomes depend so much on our own actions. I believe we all have the choice to either stop in our tracks and delay getting any relief, or move forward and manage our difficulties. I help my clients acquire coping skills to do just that.

Life keeps going, no matter what's thrown our way. We can't just stop doing what we know we need to do. Challenges are opportunities to learn and grow. The pain and discomfort from these challenges can force us to move forward, or it can cripple us.

We all experience ups and downs, but the choices you make will help you navigate them. Getting the help you need is good self-care and a smart choice. Whether that's relationship counseling or counseling to manage depression and anxiety, there's no shame in talking to a therapist. After ruling out any physiological problems, you might even opt to try a medication that assists with the counseling process. That's a decision you can make with your healthcare provider.

Where It Started for Me

I wanted to write this book because so many of you have gone through life not knowing what you want. I was the same. I grew up in a family and culture where independence was not encouraged. As a result of that, I didn't become independent until many years after reaching the legal age of eighteen. Even at twenty-one, I still behaved like a dependent minor. I never lived in my own place before marriage. I hid behind the fear that I couldn't afford to live on my own, or the excuse that I wanted to save money. I lacked the courage to do what I know I wanted, and that was to launch from my parents' home to one of my own. Yet I did the "sensible" thing and waited until I married, even though I knew living on my own was important in becoming an adult.

Even after I was married and had my own home, I went to my parents' house almost daily. My first husband attended law school in the evenings, and after my workday I would go to my parents' home before returning to my own. I thought that was normal. I worked a job that I was told would "do me well" and pay the bills, instead of something that I was passionate about.

To tell you the truth, I wasn't passionate about anything. I went through life after high school listening to what my parents said and did pretty much what they wanted me to do. Looking back, I believe I was depressed in college.

Life had changed from what I was accustomed to with my core friends in high school, and it was hard watching them venture into their own bright futures.

I was social in high school. I was a cheerleader and somewhat of a leader within my own circle of people. I had a false sense of confidence, but pulled it off quite well, which opened many doors for me when I wanted something. I was ambitious, but afraid. Intellectually, I knew what I wanted, but I didn't know what that looked or emotionally felt like.

I finished college in fewer than four years. My parents wanted me to go into nursing, because it was what was familiar to them and, again, stable and secure. By this time, though, I had started the process of listening to myself. I went into a completely different field, recreation administration with an emphasis in therapeutics. In hindsight, my gut was telling me to become a therapist, as I enjoyed helping people with their relationships.

But after I graduated, I once again took the road of least resistance: a government job that my mother believed was stable and secure. I worked that job for seven years, and I did well. I had a great work ethic and made some good friends.

I got married after I finished college. That was what I was supposed to do. I did the first-marriage route with all its trials and tribulations and had a beautiful daughter, which made all of it worth the journey.

But unbeknownst to me at the time, I had married for

the wrong reasons. Nine years later I was divorced and in the trenches of regaining and reestablishing the life I wanted. I got into graduate school with the help of a student loan and earned a master's degree in counseling psychology. I worked another stable job with the county as a social worker while obtaining my state license to practice as a psychotherapist.

Seven years with the county served as my stepping stone to a private practice as a marriage and family therapist. This was a scary and high-anxiety time. I was leaving a secure job for the unknown. Becoming a business owner in private practice really required the six steps (which I didn't have back then) to know myself. I agonized about the transition. My daughter was ten years old at the time, and I had done well to provide stability and security for us while her father was in prison.

When processing this transition with me, my therapist asked a poignant question that has become the crux for answering all difficult questions for me regarding change. He asked, "Do you have any evidence from your past showing you wanted to do something, did it, and it turned out poorly?"

I thought about everything I had done in life up until that point, and I *knew* then I had become successful because of the changes I made.

My late brother once asked me, "Whenever you say you want something, you get it. Whenever you say you want to do something, you do it. How do you do that?"

I believe, on a gut level, I had been going through the six steps all my life.

Intuition helped me get a solid sense of what I wanted. I needed courage because of conflict between what I was taught growing up and the impossibility of living that and being happy. My rollercoaster emotions created some physical and psychological problems, but while feeling the discomfort of the bad feelings, I gained insight through the process of information gathering. Because I worked on developing a greater sense of self and being less codependent, I set good limits and boundaries to become grounded, which helped me make the choices (and scary choices they were!) that were right for me.

From now on, my life is on me. Now it's your turn.

The Journey Has Already Begun

I can relate to many of you who walk through my office door, and I believe I can help you get the relief you are looking for. In working through each chapter, you too can achieve and manifest your destiny.

My hope for you is that you'll experience an incredible breakthrough as you embark on this journey with me. I've used my process of learning about myself to help other people through my practice. I hope that the stories I've shared here will help you also. I'd love for you to contact me and share your experience in reading this book, as well as what other areas you want to talk about. Please go to my website at https://couplescounselorsandiego.com to contact me or sign up for my "In The Know" publications.

At the end of the day, we're not our history. We are the relationship that we choose, and the power of a happy relationship is in our hands like never before. And when you know what you want, then go and get it.

You've done the hard work of getting to know your adult self, your *me*. Now, it's time to find the partner of your dreams, so you can create your experience of a satisfying, fulfilling relationship, your *we*.

Remember, your relationship is counting on you to become happy *me* happy *we*.

Your possibilities are endless.

ABOUT THE AUTHOR

Sarah Ruggera is a licensed marriage and family therapist and affair recovery specialist who has helped over two thousand couples, families, and individuals navigate the challenges of their relationships. She has been in private practice since 1994, has transformed from traditional psychotherapy using standardized psychotherapeutic techniques to a more dynamic, results-oriented therapy that focuses on teaching and implementing innovative tools for stronger relationships and communication.

Ruggera obtains yearly training and education far beyond the state requirements, knowing the best way to support her clients is to keep abreast of the newest techniques to help maintain and repair relationships effectively. Her San Diego–based practice is enhanced through specialized training with leaders in the relationship field.

Through Ruggera's two marriages—the second one a healthy and loving marriage of more than twenty years—and with the success of her blended family, she has learned the power of knowing oneself first, before creating a relationship with a romantic partner.

Made in the USA
Columbia, SC
17 October 2022

69564974R00087